STANDING *VICTORIOUSLY* IN THE BATTLE

~ Demystifying Spiritual Warfare

DEE BROWN

STANDING VICTORIOUSLY IN THE BATTLE
~ Demystifying Spiritual Warfare
by Dee Brown

Printed in the United States of America

ISBN 978-1-60266-489-0

All Scripture quotations, unless indicated, are taken from the New American Standard Bible, © 1980,1962,2968,1972, 1973,1975 and 1977 by the Lockman Foundation.

The Delegates of the Oxford University Press and the Syndics of the Cambridge University Press. Scripture marked NEB are taken from the New English Bible. © 1961 and 1970.

www.xulonpress.com

Dedication

I affectionately dedicate this book to the many people who came to Cornerstone Coaching and sought help for their broken hearts, souls and mind. They pressed through their pain towards personal victory.

I have grieved with, and learned from, those who could not find their way back to basic daily living and sadly some chose death to relieve their pain. I honor those who risked fears, rejection, injustices and vulnerability and those who have cried themselves to sleep. I honor you, who risk it all in an effort to be set free. Words can never do justice for the tools I have learned from walking alongside so many of you.

I give the ultimate praise to El Shaddai (The Almighty God), Jesus (Emanuel) and the Holy Spirit who has guided, equipped, and convicted me. The trinity has taught me the truth about the enemy, about myself, and ultimately the character of God. These truths have equipped me to journey with others and pass on a message of hope.

I give special honor to my mother (Maee) who encouraged me to write out the knowledge of the spiritual journey. I thank her for the rich spiritual legacy. I give thanks to my Dad for his support and teaching me to pursue my dreams. I honor my daughter, whose tender, discerning and merciful heart speaks words of affirmation and wisdom at times when I may want to give up on my own journey. My son who inspires me to minister to the broken, even from the very first time he brought lost, confused and misunderstood youth to our home. I especially honor and love my husband for his understanding in the countless nightly hours spent on this project.

Thanks to the many people who prayed, edited and labored with me to accomplish writing this book. I appreciate my dear ones: Judy, Kim, Elinor and Sherri, who spent countless hours in prayer, and the service of this project. Especially Kim, who designed and edited my first spiritual warfare workbook.

Finally, I want to give a special dedication in memory of, and love for, D.W.

Acknowledgment

Many people have contributed to the creation of this book. However, I would be remiss, if I did not specifically acknowledge Pastor Diane Altman. Her loving and tireless dedication has been an inspiration and the reason this book is now complete. Diane supported, and encouraged me from the beginning of this holy assignment. She spent countless hours hammering and fine-tuning the content as she utilized her editing and journalism skills. Pastor Diane's commitment and professionalism are a special gift to me personally. She spent time seeking the heart of God to make sure the book was anointed and guided by Him. Diane has helped me to put feet to the truth expressed in this material. She has battled the enemy and stood victoriously to see that this material would "go forth." I am extremely proud to have such a creative and accountable friend to walk this journey with me through the last four years. I thank her entire family for releasing her to assist me in this spiritual journey.

Contents

Introduction:

Demystifying Spiritual Warfare

I am compelled to write this material for women. Though the tailored message is specific to fit the needs of women, the content is genderless. It is my prayer that the truths expressed will assist you in discovering the nature of the one against whom we war. There is an enemy, known by most as Satan. He is real and he is waging an intense battle for the heart, mind, soul and spirit of all humanity. He is an ancient, cunning, strategic, deceptive, and diabolical foe.

Equipping women to live in the light of eternity and receive the grace and love of Father God is my life calling. For years, the Lord has planted seeds of simplistic, yet practical, tools to utilize when standing boldly in the spiritual battles. These tools were revealed as I walked alongside people in their battles.

The strategic design of this material will give women a practical understanding of spiritual warfare. God has been very clear in His Word. We have the information we need to stand victoriously. Regardless of our personal situations, we can learn to walk effectively and triumphantly. I am excited to share these tools.

At the end of each chapter, I have included reflection questions for you to begin using the tools you gain while reading the book. This is not specifically a devotional book; however, experience at conferences and in using this material with a multitude of women I have found personal devotion to the Lord inevitably grows during the journey. So take this opportunity to seek the heart of God for your circumstances. You may want to use a separate journal to expand your thoughts and reflect on each question in detail.

God explains all we need to know about Satan in six main areas in Scripture. These areas point us to the tools we must apprehend as we walk equipped through the battles of life. God reveals Satan's specific spiritual warfare attacks; on Heaven, in the Garden of Eden and in the wilderness with Jesus. First, God tells us Satan declared war on His heavenly family. Second, scripture records how the enemy acted on that declaration and attacked God's earthly family. Third, the word reveals Satan's plan and the attack on Jesus, God's Son. Satan understood that Jesus' death and resurrection was the redemptive plan of God to defeat him. Fourth, God gives us strategic tools by disclosing the tactical characteristics of the enemy, through descriptive names He ascribes to Satan. Fifth, God tells us who we are, and exactly what authority we possess in Christ Jesus as His beloved children. Our Heavenly Father, God, desires to lavish on us as beloved daughters. Sixth, God reveals His own attributes and strategies to help us in the warfare.

This material will demystify spiritual warfare by examining and exposing you to six areas in Biblical Scripture. You will also gain an understanding of how God's names incorporate a promise and are a tactical spiritual warfare tool. In this process you will be empowered, equipped and enriched, allowing you to live with greater expectancy, truth and triumph.

Why am I so passionate about this book? It comes from my own valley journey and desperation to demystify spiritual warfare. Additionally, my calling is to communicate tools that equip people to live abundant lives free from the snares of the enemy.

God tells us when we have done all we can to stand in life's battles, we are to remember His truth which affirms He has already won the war and defeated Satan. Our heavenly Father, God, promises to fight the daily battles for us. Claiming and declaring God's promises allows us to stand strong in the very eye of battle storms. This does not mean standing helplessly while the war rages. Instead, apply Biblical wisdom and stand armed and dangerous no matter what the enemy unleashes. I want to say here and now, no weapon formed against you will prosper. You must choose to stand on a solid foundation and activate God's truth in your life.

In my many years as a nurse and private practice counselor, there were times I could hardly catch my breath after viewing the devastation in people's eyes and lives. Some of the tragedy resulted from their own decisions, generational choices, or patterns of behavior. Many have fallen prey to Satan from lack of knowledge and wisdom. Others did not have people in their lives to speak honestly with love. By listening to the Holy Spirit, I began to see the road to living a victorious life. There is a pathway in the midst of life's storms. I know, through the power of Christ, people can shatter strongholds and bondages. Satan has no power other than what we give him, or what God's sovereign will permits. God can, and will, change us from the inside out.

This book answers practical questions as it demystifies evil, allowing us to stand strong in the battles and live in freedom.

Part I

ARMED TO STAND UP

Chapter 1

God's Beloved Daughters

"The Lord will perfect and accomplish what concerns me; your loving-kindness, O Lord, is everlasting; do not abandon nor forsake the works of your hands." *(Psalm 138:8)*

As the sun warmed her body, she knew her soul needed warmth also. She looked at the nearby flower with wonder. If God could create such a glorious rose, surely He had a plan in creating her. She had experienced many of life's thorns, but the overall fragrance of her life was still sweet. Then, she remembered the words that had changed her perspective. These words were "Even if you are a desert flower in the driest place, bloom, baby, bloom." Yes, God did have a plan and purpose for her life and the bouquet was not yet complete.

There is a divine plan and purpose for each person God created. However, today we see tremendous pain in the eyes of women all around the world. Women do not realize who they really are in God's eyes. So many women long for restoration and full health. Countless women have asked God for healing and have felt abandoned when the healing is not apparent. Others do not know where to begin to untangle the past and step into the future with boldness and freedom.

Mind-boggling thoughts of shame, fear, unworthiness, failure, discontentment and false guilt bombard today's woman. Television, movies and magazines depict women as sexual objects. Often a woman's looks, size, age, clothing, and marital status become a quick calculation of worth. This leaves so much of society unfulfilled and confused. Women try to conform to these images. However, buying into these views will leave us empty and lacking in self-worth and confidence. When there is a sense of barrenness, it is tempting to hide. To hide those feelings behind religion, food, addictions, emotional affairs or unhealthy relationships is a common occurrence. This is not God's plan for the precious daughters of His kingdom.

God wants us to rise above images because we are created in His image. In Genesis, we learn that, "in His image God created him, male and female." We must begin to see ourselves through the reflection of God's eyes. God has uniquely created each of us and He likes diversity. Just as no two snowflakes are alike, neither are any two people completely alike. When we try to think, act and dress like every other woman; we are erasing the beautiful painting God made into each one of us. We are valued and are worth the fight. Ladies, we are far greater than the most precious jewels. Because of this fact, God will contradict our circumstances, help us gain victory in our lives and ultimately complete the destiny He has prepared for each one of us. God wants to bless us and in turn, we are able to bless others.

You must know the Lord loves deeply and rejoices with your victories. When there are hardships, He is still on the journey. The name of God, called El Roi, means the God who sees you. First Peter 2:9 says we are a chosen people, a royal priesthood, a holy nation, a people belonging to God, and we may declare the praises of Him who called you. God chose you! This verse allows you to know what God sees in His daughters. You are able to have confidence in God as it says in Ephesians chapter 3 verse 12. "We have a boldness and confidence from an intimate connection through our faith in God." Women must see themselves as being wonderfully made. In Eph. 2:10 it states, "For we are God's workmanship, created in Christ Jesus to do good works in the world." This is especially important for women who struggle with perfectionist tendencies and never feel they measure up to a high standard. The pursuit of perfection and approval drives us farther from peace and self-confidence. God is not looking for you to perform and try to win His favor. The Heavenly Father's love comes from His grace and mercy towards all women. You cannot earn God's love through works because God imparts His love freely because of grace. Yet, women still struggle with listening to too many outside voices. There are internal and external voices that dictate the path we walk. Breaking free from the things that serve to bind and entrap you will clarify the right road to take. You can step into the plan designed especially for you by God Himself.

Whatever the mission and dream, we must fulfill them. Each of us has a journey to walk out. Even the pain on the path is part of the process of maturing and growing us into Christ's likeness. If we let the Lord use our trials and tribulations, the gates of hell cannot prevail or stop what the Lord wants to fulfill in, around and through us. The healing process we go through may be what another person needs to hear in their steps to freedom and wholeness. If you are willing to stay in the journey and stand in the battle, you will not be alone. Our Father will not forsake you. Let the peace of Christ Jesus rule your heart.

There are seasons when friends, family or support people may not be available. You know what I mean. There are times in the midnight hours, when your mind will not turn off the events from the day or previous days. In these times, hopelessness and depression may grip your very soul. Dear ones, the Lord is still awake and is ready to listen, comfort and fight the battles. Do not give in or give up, my sister. Keep it real by staying out of denial, but instead stand boldly on the truth of who you are. Romans chapter 8 verse 37, reminds us we are more than conquerors through Him who loves us. You must align yourself with the truth of the word.

Although, as women, there is a tendency to feel alone and lonely at times, the Lord will allow people to come into our life to stand in the gap. Some will pray or listen, while others may provide Godly counsel or the completion of daily practical tasks. The Lord will move in peoples' lives to quicken their hearts to assist us by serving in certain times in our lives. However, if people do not reach out to you, take the risk and ask for help. God also provides angels who come alongside to strengthen and remind us of the hope and future that is ours in Christ Jesus.

God wants to heal, renew and restore. By continuing to seek God's plans for our life, we will stand battle focused and armored in the storms of life. We will move away from areas where we can become confused, bruised, battered, disgusted and busted. We will not hide behind religion, addictions, food or unhealthy relationships when we embrace the truth about ourselves.

The enemy of our souls seeks to slander our name, lie to us, distort our thinking and destroy our destiny. The enemy will try to kill our hopes and dreams. Sometimes, the enemy throws so much drama at us that we don't know which way to turn. During these times, it is important to cry out, "Lord, have mercy." I have discovered our heavenly Father has given us power to choose the way we respond to the drama. When drama happens, we must ask what we need to learn through the season. Sisters, we are standing tall in a battle. To stand tall, sometimes we have to straighten up and know it is time to walk in the truth of your destiny. We can stand for God's purposes because we have the gift of choice. Therefore, you can choose this day to serve and stand on the winning side of the battle. Satan does not want you to claim or walk empowered with the gift of choice.

Sometimes we need to remember how Jesus already paid the price for anything we will ever do, have done, think we might do, ought to have done, or need to do. He already paid for all of our sins by His blood shed on the battlefield. Because of that truth, who you are, were, or hope to become does not shock God. He is not impatient with the fact that you are in the process of maturing. He is forever the Alpha and Omega, which means the beginning and the end. He has the time for us as we fully develop into Christ-like people. God will give us the time if you will take it.

We must tell ourselves, "The Lord loves me just as I am", which is a great place to start the maturing process. Otherwise, I have seen the enemy tell people they have to have it all together before seeking the Lord's help. There is power in the process and passion in the purpose. You are already a success if you chose to stand with the Lord and not run away, hoping things will be better.

In the Bible, the book of Luke chapter 8 tells a story of a woman with no name who made a choice to be free even at a great risk. The Bible tells us this woman with the issue of blood dealt with rejection, abandonment, slander and isolation from society. She was unclean according to the standards of the times. Physicians of the day could not restore her health. People did not understand and did not support her in her despair. This woman was crushed and broken, yet she was not destroyed. She decided to activate her faith by facing fears and pursuing her healing. She emerges from the story a free woman after years of suffering. For the times, she did something radical just coming out in public with such a misunderstood condition.

When we need a miracle, we can choose to seize miracle moments in our lives. We must not slumber and miss the seasons of miracles. It takes a bit of faith to believe in a dream, a hope and the future. When we pursue the miracles, God moves all of heaven on our behalf. Even the smallest amount of faith, the size of a mustard seed, can bring about miracles.

Anytime we have a need that is greater than our resources, we have entered into a miracle season. There are times in our lives when we are in over our heads and a sick feeling lodges in the pit of our stomach. Dear ones, watch out in these times, because a miracle season has arrived. Satan wants us to stay in that powerless place. However, God will pull us up as we acknowledge that in our weaknesses He is strong. He will not let you drown in a sea of fears, regrets and discouragement. God promises He will hold you up when you feel weak. The truth is, when you are at the end of your strength, it is the beginning of God's strength.

It is important to know, when we need our friends, and no one is home. When we need a healing touch from the Lord and no one understands. When we have a season where we need deliverance. We must learn to press into the battle and hold onto even the smallest grasp of faith and claim the promises from God.

Therefore, we must hold our faith high because this is the day the Lord has made for us. It is possible to walk with our heads held high. When the weight of shame, fear and doubts lift, our eyes can look towards heaven and receive comfort and mercy. Yes, we may experience heartaches in life. However, we do not need to linger encumbered by life's burdens. By reading this book now, you have already begun a journey into living a victorious life. This is your day, hour, moment or season. It is time to break the chains of bondage and pull down every manner of stronghold. If you have been holding back, allow the Holy Spirit to take you through a long awaited release. As women, we have the opportunity to experience freedom from things that ensnare and prevent us from growing. We are standing in the battle as precious daughters of the King of Kings. God will give us the strength to stand up, straighten our backs and hold our heads up high. Praise God! The Word tells us in Psalm chapter 31 verse 1 to bless the Lord at all times. We can overcome all things and live abundant lives. Right now, you are learning what you need to stand strong, solid and true wherever you are on the path of life.

Chapter 1 *God's Beloved Daughters ~ Reflection*

1. In what ways can you see yourself as a daughter of the King of Kings?

2. When you were a little girl, did you ever imagine yourself as a princess? Why or why not? Was there a person in your life who helped you feel beautiful or possibly someone who stole that feeling from you?

3. Do you understand God wants you to take a rightful identity as His daughter with royal blood? How does that make you feel?

Journal Notes ~ Write your additional thoughts on how you can daily see yourself as a daughter of the King of Kings.

Chapter 2
Satan Declares War

"For though we live in the world, we do not wage war as the world does. The weapons we fight with are not the weapons of the world. On the contrary, they have divine power to demolish strongholds. Casting down arguments and every high thing that exalts itself against the knowledge of God. Bringing every thought into captivity to the obedience of Christ." *(2 Corinthians 10:3-5)*

Her head hung down and eyes searched the floor as she pushed back the tears. She began to tell of the many things she had experienced in her life and how it led to continual pain. As the words tumbled from her lips, a smile seemed far from possible. However, this daughter of the King would smile again. She learned through her journey what we all must know: God has a divine plan for all his children as described in the Bible in the book of Jeremiah chapter 29 verse 11.

Recognizing there is a war raging around us and we are in the battle, is the first step of standing in the battle. Declare what Jesus tells us in Matthew chapter 28 verse 18, when He says, "All authority in heaven and on earth has been given to us." The following statements will serve to demystify the spiritual warfare journey so you will be stronger. Spiritual warfare is defined as the battle waged in the unseen spiritual realm, which is revealed in the natural physical realm. Spiritual warfare is a proactive approach to releasing our faith in any circumstance. That may seem difficult to understand now, but this book is purposely clear. It will bring victory to your life as you gain greater under-standing of the nature of spiritual warfare. Sisters, as you gain clarity reading this book, and apply God's principles to your life, I guarantee you will move from sitting down and feeling like a powerless victim, to standing firm in whatever battles you face and knowing you can live in victory.

Everyone has a choice of two paths; one led by the enemy and the other by God. The enemy's path is full of bondage, fear, apathy, confusion, condemnation, defeat, indifference and false security. God's path leads to peace, intercession, influence, reconciliation, abundance, discernment, healing, renewal, mercy, acceptance, and trust crowned with humility. The obvious contrast between God's way and Satan's way is striking and it is a real spiritual battle for hearts, minds and souls. Our Heavenly Father gives us the gift of choice. You are obviously choosing the path of righteousness through Christ Jesus. Your choice to pick up this book and persevere in the journey of understanding proves the path you are choosing.

The Abba Father is constantly wooing us all to take steps out of pain and into freedom. When we step out in His name, faith moves in our lives. To be free enough to be all that you are intended to become is to be free indeed. Nevertheless, Satan wants to deceive people onto the path he creates.

The traits of the enemy are clear. Darkness, deception, divisiveness, distortion, distraction, deflection and destruc-tion are his trademarks. We know, however, God already dethroned the enemy. As princess warriors, we are to be alert to the schemes of the enemy. We are not to become fearful or paranoid. We do not need to go out of our way looking for demonic activity, but when we encounter it, we can learn to recognize it. Then we are able to confront it with spiritual authority given to us by the Lord. The Bible tells us in Isaiah 41:10 to not be afraid and that our God will strengthen us, help us, and upholds us through all of life's adversities. Therefore, now is not a time to be timid in proclaiming who we are in Christ Jesus. Seek God's face and develop an intimate walk with Him. When we practice a walk of faith through obedient actions, God adds to our strength.

The challenge is when life's battles begin to rage and it is tempting to fight with the people around us. Soon, our fathers, husbands, brothers, sisters, co-workers or those who cross our path become fair game for our frustration. However, the true battle is with the enemy of our souls. We must unveil the strategy of the enemy of all humanity and demystify the tactics of spiritual warfare. The first step is to examine the battle plan and to study the initial attacks of Satan. Each attack unveils a deliberate strategy used by Satan to entrap and separate humanity from God.

The Heavenly Attack

The original battle with Satan began in Heaven. By understanding the heavenly strategy of deception used before our creation, we set ourselves up to be victorious warriors in the battle. God has already won the war. However, we must learn to walk in this war and through the daily battles. Ezekiel chapter 28 reveals the battle does not really have to do with us, but rather, with Satan's status as an anointed cherub in Heaven. It has to do with his ultimate fall from grace. The fall of Satan was due to pride, power and jealousy. This pride and desire for power allowed him to challenge God. The enemy wanted to be God and maintain control of the kingdoms of this world. Because of the enemy's desire for control and his influential abilities, he convinced one third of the angelic beings to leave heaven and become his followers. We know these followers as demons. In declaring war on God and all of humanity, Satan and his followers created division in heaven. Not only did Satan cause division, but also he devises destructive plans to carry out daily on earth. These battle plans are what develop into spiritual warfare. The significance of the original events alerts us that the enemy was not afraid of God then and he is not afraid of you now. However, the enemy does tremble when we walk in the light of truth through Jesus Christ. Make no mistake: we are in a strategic war.

The truth is the enemy has become more cunning over the passage of time. Nevertheless, it is important to grasp the truth that Satan's strategic plans remain the same today. Unveiling those strategies gives us an awareness of what Satan is capable of doing in our lives. It also empowers us to prevent Satan from taking spiritual ground in our lives. The same enemy, who allowed pride and defiance to separate him from his creator, God, also seeks to have us choose the identical destructive path. Second Corinthians 2:11 says do not be caught "unaware of the schemes of Satan". The enemy wants us to rely only on ourselves and to believe we are incompetent, insignificant and that God is not for us. Satan's goal is to keep unbelievers in the dark. He also wants to prevent believers from bringing glory to God. The enemy has attempted to hinder the work of God on earth. The enemy knows God is our power source in obtaining the wisdom for victory in spiritual battles. Satan wants us to be imprisoned captives. He desires to use us as a pawn for him in obtaining more and more power.

Many ask, if Satan is defeated, why do spiritual wars rage in our lives? There two answers to this question. As with any war, there are soldiers who are determined to win and will always resist defeat. They refuse to give up or allow their enemy to take territory. Satan knows he is defeated, but refuses to surrender. Secondly, once we know how to resist the enemy's tactics we can become spiritual warriors with authority as followers of Jesus Christ. I am not going to say this is easy, because Satan will waltz right on into your house, job, and ministry. However, when you recognize the attacks in your life, you can draw on Scripture to stand strong and persevere. Warfare teaches us how to endure as victors and not victims. Take note, this is a spiritual war and cannot be won by natural means. It always requires spiritual weapons. It requires spiritual eyesight to see the battle and determine the specific tactics so you can respond accordingly. Throughout this book, weapons will be continually unveiled so you will see the tools used to stand in victory.

The Earthly Attack

Satan's second attack was in the Garden of Eden, where he appeared as a serpent to Eve. The garden tactic is a story of deceptive enticement, shame, blame and division. He convinced Eve to disobey God and eat the fruit from the tree of knowledge of good and evil. In the Book of Genesis chapter 3, Satan, as the serpent, used the tactics of deception and temptation. He deceitfully enticed Eve by distorting God's words and insinuating doubt about the character of God. From then, to this day, if we have wrong beliefs about God, it is an inroad from the enemy to our heart and mind. Because of the serpent's tactic, Eve believed God was withholding knowledge, wisdom and truth.

When people directly attack us, our first reaction may be to defend ourselves. When we are tempted, we have the ability to make a choice. Satan loves to mess with our minds. A thought becomes a belief. Based on that belief system, we make a choice. If the choice is seeded and rooted in lies or distortions, an unhealthy habit forms. Without light shed on the habit, it will become a stronghold. Any unchecked and unhealed strongholds become bondage. When women find themselves in a stronghold or bondage, they frequently isolate themselves because of fear, unrealistic expectations or shame. It is essential for women to break the isolation by finding people who are safe enough to listen without judgment. Trusted people become ones who hold each another accountable through the process of becoming healthy. This relationship only works if people are willing and are strong enough to risk speaking the truth with love.

It does not take much experience to see how the enemy tempts people. For example, we can work hard to have an amazingly healthy garden around us by cultivating quality friendships and receiving bouquets of blessings. Yet, in that garden, weeds such as fear, disappointment, shame, blame, discontentment, rejection, and abuse can choke out the joy in our lives. These same weeds grow deep in our hearts and take root if we do not know how to heal and renew our mind. That is when you are experiencing the enemy's garden tactics. It is essential to realize the same experiences plagued our ancestors throughout their life journey. Even though, the surroundings and times were different, the seed of deception Satan uses to produce weeds and thorns remain unchanged. Understanding that truth alone gives hope because when we know the tactics of an enemy, we can be proactive.

Satan also utilized the tactic of divisiveness in the Garden of Eden. Adam stood by and watched Eve disobey God. He did not protect her in a priestly way, as God had instructed. After Eve and Adam ate the fruit and received knowledge of good and evil, all hell broke loose on earth. When God came to visit them and called their names, they were both afraid. In the book of Genesis chapter 3, we see the plan of Satan unfold. When God questioned Adam as to what had happened, blame and shame entered the world. Adam blamed God for giving him the woman. Eve blamed the serpent. As a woman, can you imagine having a sweet, honest, open relationship with God and your husband? Then, all of a sudden, accusations hit you, which pierce your heart to the core. Can you picture how that woman must have felt? I dare say, at the very least, she would have experienced emotions of betrayal, rejection, shame, mistrust, guilt and fear. This struggle between men and women continues to this day. One way to be victorious in this struggle is to confront issues as quickly as possible, so the enemy does not gain a foothold. Secondly, as we develop an intimate walk with the Lord, we can count on Him to direct and guide our path. Also, surrender to the will of the Lord by acknowledging His Sovereignty. Lastly, practice obedience in living out the truth of God on this earth, until we reach our heavenly home.

Consequences followed Adam, Eve and the serpent's actions. God disciplined them all. Our Abba Father loves us. Therefore, like any father who loves his children, there is discipline given. Scriptures tell us to be watchful of our thought life and what gets buried in our hearts. Be careful of the choices you make in life. Nonetheless, no matter what mistakes or sins are committed, God provides a way to turn around. God looks at the motive of our hearts and not our weaknesses and failures. God is faithful to forgive you and continues to love you with His everlasting love. He also gives the gift of peace, which passes all human reason. The key to freedom is to admit the truth, ask God for forgiveness, forgive yourself and step out of shame and pain. Remember, it is a process.

The Wilderness Attack

Satan's third attack was in the wilderness with Jesus as described in the book of Matthew chapter four. Jesus was not exempt from Satan's attacks. Satan strategically attacked Jesus during His season of depleted basics of life such as food, water and support. He waited until Jesus was vulnerable. Satan began using the tactic of tempting Jesus with all possible desires. Satan offered Him many options to walk away from God. Every time the enemy tried to tempt Jesus, the only spiritual warfare tool Jesus used was the Word of His Father, stating ". . . It is written". Jesus did not debate or argue with Satan. Jesus knew the truth of the word and spoke the word to resist the enemy. Jesus wants us to do the same. It is also essential for you to realize that even though the enemy fled at the time, he also waited for another opportunity. In our lives, those opportune times of temptation come when we feel we are in a valley. Satan also comes to tempt right after we have just experienced something great, like a mountain top experience. Remember, this season of temptation for Jesus came immediately after His public baptism. Satan uses these valley and mountain experiences because his goal is to rob, steal and destroy. Understanding these truths allows you to be watchful, so you do not leave yourselves open for an attack.

All humans have basic fundamental needs to belong, have significance, feel worthy, and experience competence. If a sense of personal value is lacking, feelings of inferiority set-in. If a sense of belonging is absent, insecurity sets-in. If a sense of vision and purpose is missing, insignificance and illegitimacy set-in. If there is a sense of incompetence, people feel inadequate and devalued.

Women may seek arenas to build personal identity through works especially in a competitive world. If that occurs, it causes us to fall into the enemy's deceptive traps.

It is essential that we base our esteem and value on our creation as daughters of the Most High God, not on our actions that can lead to striving and self-sufficiency. When we have our identity in Christ, we will defeat and prevent the enemy's heavenly tactic of false pride and self-sufficiency from becoming our downfall. Sisters, when we ask the Lord to be our Savior, we have the Holy Spirit come into our lives. Imagine, the Holy Spirit taking up residence in us. Do you realize that means wherever you tread in this world, that you bring the Holy Spirit power with you? The good news is, in Christ, we have all authority to stand in the war until the final defeat of the enemy.

Frequently, women are tempted in wilderness seasons. The enemy will attempt to capitalize on any perceived, or real, weaknesses and vulnerabilities. Such vulnerabilities include isolation, desolation, discontentment, physical shortcomings, and emotional unmet needs. If we feel alienated or far from God, we may find our wilderness season seems full of temptations. These vulnerabilities still affect women all over the world and continue to be entry tactics for Satan. When women feel lack in their basic needs, they may compromise themselves to obtain what is missing. They may surround themselves with people who provide empty compliments or dishonest relationships. Young women, for example, may be tempted to align themselves with someone who seems like a good provider. They make the mistake of jumping quickly into a long-term relationship believing it will fill the hole of insecurity in their heart. That impulsive decision may not be God's best for their destiny.

When a woman fills the empty holes in her heart, without waiting on God to provide the answers, she often comes up with the short end of the stick. Holes in the heart can develop from trauma or be the outcome of an unhealthy family. These experiences foster patterns of distorted thinking. Eventually, she may become a survivor attempting to protect herself from further hurts. People are born with a survivor instinct and some need to cope with continual pain to prevent further emotional and relational hurt because of their environment. Sisters, no matter what the environment, we must know that our Father God desires to give everyone a sense of worth, belonging, purpose and competence. Rise up, take ownership and walk out onto the path of freedom.

In understanding tactics of the enemy, we become aware how free will allows us to choose. We can choose a journey full of peace and freedom or one of despair and defeat. Hear me, victory does not necessarily mean we will be devoid of trials and tribulation. What it does mean, is we will know how to respond when the enemy hits us with his tactics. We can walk out of the wilderness to a place of full grace and freedom in God's love. By Jesus' example in the wilderness, we see the path to walk out of temptation victoriously.

Though the heavenly, garden and wilderness tactics of the enemy appear different, they all have the same goal and each one reveals the enemy's tactic. Satan's goal is to keep non-believers from obtaining a personal relationship with God. He also attempts to keep believers ineffective or immobilized in reaching out to others or fulfilling their destiny. Satan's desire is to devour. The root definition of the word "devour" is "to swallow". He will attempt to get you so swamped that you are busy with spiritually unproductive living instead of basking in an abundant life. Exchange your fear for faith and turn helplessness into hope. Replace any lie with the truth. Claim the promises of God. I have certain scriptures that I run to in the midst of trouble, such as Isaiah chapter 61. God uses those scriptures to comfort me, direct me and reassure me. There are times specific scriptural verses will lead me to the very truth I need to deal with my circumstance. At other times, memorizing scripture renews my mind. Hebrews 10:

16 lets us know that God wants His precepts, truth and promises to live in our hearts and minds. When truth is living in us, the Holy Spirit can revive just what we need because of previous deposits in our hearts and minds.

Knowing the enemy's tactics, goals and understanding God's power means we can ultimately have victory. These truths equip us in walking restored, freed, transformed and released to become all God originally intended, while bringing glory to His kingdom. Then we treat those who cross our path as divine appointments and are blessed by our testimony rather than frustrated in our test.

Essentially, with the Word of God, prayer, truth and relationally safe people walking alongside us, we are able to move away from a defeated place as a victim. We can then live as a victor and embrace the grace and love of our heavenly Father. Then we see that ultimately, the battle belongs to the Lord, and we are truly able to stand strong, persevere through the battle and live equipped even in the midst of the war. Remember, Satan cannot take anything away from us that God cannot redeem.

Chapter 2 *Satan Declares War~ Reflection*

1. In what ways have you seen God's love in your life?

2. When you first felt a painful conflict in your life, what was the origin of that battle? Can you identify a certain experience or person who created the conflict?

3. Do you know God wants to take you out of pain and into His fullest freedom? How does that make you feel?

Journal Notes ~ Write your additional thoughts about times you may have experienced the enemy's attempts to deceive or immobilize you. Also, declare some statements about what you hope to gain from continuing to stand in the battle.

Chapter 3

Unveiling the Enemy

"Some people are like seed along the path, where the word is sown. As soon as they hear it, Satan comes and takes away the word that was sown in them." *(Mark 4:15)*

Leaving the conference, she knew she would do better with her life. She had enjoyed the praise music, camaraderie with other women, food she did not have to prepare and the messages had been informative and surprisingly entertaining. She had not known what to expect from the women's conference, but she enjoyed the pause from her regular busy paced life. Yes, now she felt renewed and ready to take on her new opportunities to live as a solid young Christian. However, as she entered her car, the cell phone rang and the challenges of daily life greeted her. The further she drove from the conference, the more her trials seemed to apprehend her. It seemed the peace, joy, and praise she experienced would quickly become a memory as her road twisted back to her usual path.

In the Book of Mark, Jesus tells us that Satan comes to steal the truth from us. However, if we grab onto the idea that we have a tremendous amount of power to take back what he steals, we will be empowered.

God unveils the enemy by giving him names, which spotlight his character traits and his tactics of war. The names God gives Satan are weapons in our understanding of how he will try to operate in our lives. For example, when we know someone's name, we know something about where she is from, what she answers to and we are able to identify her reputation.

We will specifically identify eleven names used in the Bible when referring to the enemy of our souls. Understanding the names God gives the enemy is a powerful strategy women can use during spiritual battles. This information becomes a tool to use when we confront the situations identified within the names. We can pull out the tools needed to bring defeat to the enemy. This gives us the ability to identify the tool we can use, name the enemy tactic and respond accordingly.

One of those tools will be to study the names of God. The names God has are descriptive of His attributes and promises, which counter the tactic of the enemy. We will address God's names in another chapter of this book. For now, as we examine the names of the enemy, realize we are moving from seated to standing. Ladies, we are taking a stand against frustration of the unknown and are taking up the tools while being empowered with every word we read. At this point, we are already demystifying spiritual warfare, standing as a daughter of the King and now we are able to unveil the names of the enemy.

The Adversary

Satan's Trait: The Adversary is an opponent with no capacity to show grace, love or mercy.

God's Truth: I am He who is El Shaddai. I am The Almighty God, who is full of grace. There is victory in Jesus Christ.

God calls Satan the adversary fifty times in biblical scripture. Whenever God uses a word more than once, we need to perk up. I have heard pastors, other believers and even myself say, "Yes, Satan is our adversary." However, I did not grasp the full thrust of the name "Adversary," until the Holy Spirit had me study deeper in the scriptures. A dictionary definition of adversary says it means "opponent, enemy, someone who is against everything good. An adversary has no capacity to show mercy." Sometimes, we call an opponent on sports teams an adversary. However, this use of the word "adversary" is far from that which God uses to name Satan. A true adversary is an enemy who is against you, not merely one competing with you. Understanding the definition itself may be a sobering view into the enemy's character.

In the Bible, First Peter 5:8 warns us how the enemy walks or roams about like a lion. When we look at the specific tactics of the enemy, we will examine the strategy of a lion on the hunt and what that may mean to us, as we understand the battle with the one called the Adversary.

The Devil

Satan's Trait: The Devil is an enemy who slanders personal identity. Satan wants you to believe you are nothing to God.

God's Truth: Your identity is in Christ. He created your inmost being. He knit you together in your mother's womb. You are wonderfully made.

If you have ever had someone attempt to attack your personhood, to slander you, create inner turmoil by berating your character, shame you, or pile on false guilt, you must now step into victory and unveil Satan the Devil. The word Devil means the one who will slander us. This is not a new method of the enemy. In fact, the Old Testament refers to slander a hundred times and the New Testament holds sixty more references of slander. Again, we must know the name of our enemy so we can defeat rather than become defeated.

The Devil, as the book of Revelation chapter 20 verse 10 calls him, will attempt to slander and defame you in an attempt to snatch your entire identity as a daughter of the King. Our significance defines our identity. If that identity, security and significance are under attack, we potentially become unsure if we even matter to God. The process of shame makes it difficult to separate a person's behavior from their person-hood. In other words when you believe what you have done is the same as who you are; it is an encounter with an enemy tactic. If the Devil is successful at attacking identity, there may be feelings of disconnect in identifying yourself, as a child of the Living God. There may also be a distortion of thinking because you see everything through lenses of shame.

A distorted lens begins with a thought and can become a belief system such as: "God is uncaring," "God is relationally distant," "God is waiting to hammer me if I do something wrong," "No matter what I do, it will never be good enough," and "God is dissatisfied with who I am and what I do." Such destructive distortions become a head game where thinking becomes like a tape playing in our mind. This method, referred to as self-talk, creates enemy inroads to minds and hearts. If these negative tapes remain uncorrected distortions, there is potential for them to progress into destructive habits, strongholds and ultimately bondage.

Distortion about God makes it difficult for some women to trust God and accept His love. It is freeing to discover the distortions and address the seeds, which have taken root. If these distortions about God remain unhealed, a door is open for the enemy to continue slandering your identity. Ladies, you must go deep and uncover the seeds of distortions in your lives. One way to begin uprooting seeds of distortion is to ask, "When did the distortion begin and how did it grow?" Ask the Holy Spirit to unveil the truth. Do not be afraid to ask for help. You may need it to uncover the source of the distortions.

Abaddon

Satan's Trait: The enemy will try to destroy you or render you ineffective in this world.

God's Truth: You have a destiny beyond yourself and forgiveness for the mistakes of the past as you walk new battleground.

Abaddon literally means destroyer and destruction. Revelations chapter 9 verse 11 refers to Satan with this terminology. Visualization is a powerful tool. Take a moment and visualize an army getting ready for battle. The entire idea of preparing for battle is to destroy the enemy. The enemy's entire preparation for battle is to bring about our destruction. Satan will do anything to see us destroyed or become immobilized so his army can take over this world. Abaddon will use family, friends, jobs, ministry, past mistakes, and past pain to bring people down. If there is no healing or learning to grieve and forgive, the enemy will resurrect these issues. The negative self-talk will continue to replay the past to destroy our present and affect our future.

Whether it is the process of destroying or the result of complete destruction, Abaddon has the goal of rendering everyone ineffective for the Kingdom of God. The enemy wants you to turn away from God as your Heavenly Father. The use of these tactics serves to abort the destiny God planned for individuals since the beginning of time. Satan desires to incapacitate people who rise-up and connect with Father God.

The process of confession is a powerful tool that many dread. However, it is part of the walk with the Father. Confession keeps life actions in the light and promotes intimacy with our heavenly Father. Years ago, the Holy Spirit, allowed me to understand how confession was a strategic warfare tool. There are two truths to embrace and activate about confession. If you fess-up to the truth in life and place it in the light for God to heal, then you beat Satan at his own con game. Confession is a powerful weapon in life because placing actions and attitudes in the light renders the enemy powerless. This strategic process allows us to speak truth to ourselves and it removes negative self-talk at the same time. God stands ready to release confessions into the ocean of forgiveness. The Bible says, He remembers no more and you have full forgiveness. However, to be completely free, you must forgive yourself. Amen!

Beelzebub

Satan's Trait: Beelzebub will feed off anything to wound. Beelzebub wants you to believe that if you have weakness, insecurity or hurts, you are destined to remain a victim.

God's Truth: Jehovah Rapha is able to heal and redeem you.

When the Pharisees in Matthew 12 verse 24 accused Jesus of driving out demons by the power of Satan called Beelzebub, it is the first time the name is used in the Bible. Beelzebub literally means the Lord of the Flies.

This reference to Satan makes sense when we consider how flies swarm, and feed off dead things. Although it is a disgusting picture, it is even worse when we consider how the enemy attempts to feed off the dead, or painful, things in our lives.

The dead things of life stem from prior events and if there is a focus on the past, it affects current choices. If the enemy feasts on these areas of hurt, guilt or shame, we potentially develop a distorted belief system that threatens to stop the plans of God in our lives.

A popular saying comes to mind, "If one of the chair legs is broken, don't keep sitting on it." Pretending it is still capable of holding weight is detrimental to health.

Ladies, you must get off the broken chair. I have observed people living a merry-go-round lifestyle. They continue to use ineffective methods expecting different results. Unhealed painful experiences can cause people to go round-and-round and up-and-down until they develop inner promises, or vows. If we do not get off the ride and heal these inner vows, the enemy, Beelzebub, will use it. For example, people make inner vows such as: "I will never let anyone love me again," "I will never be weak or powerless in the future," or "I will never need anyone." When inner vows take hold, they create an internal prison. The enemy feeds off people who hold onto areas of weakness, hurt, insecurity or shame-based thinking. The enemy does not want you to acknowledge negative thinking patterns and weakness. Psalm chapter 34 verse 19 tells us we have many afflictions in life. The Lord will deliver us from those afflictions and set us free. To find freedom, you must speak, declare and live the truth of Jesus Christ.

The Anointed Cherub

Satan's Trait: The enemy is able to imitate God's power.

God's Truth: God is all knowing, all powerful and present. God limits Satan's powers.

We read in the book of Ezekiel chapter 28 that Satan began as an anointed Cherub. We must also acknowledge the Anointed Cherub has limited power. We are informed so we see his present state and know his future. Verses 11 to 19 describe Satan as God's masterpiece. God tells us Satan had the seal of perfection and was perfect in beauty and full of wisdom. Satan was the sum total of God's creation. The key word to linger on is that he "*was.*" We know from his past that he had great ability.

In verse 14, God conveys to us the role of Satan before his fall was to serve as God's anointed Cherub. Cherubs covered the throne of God. He was the head honcho of the Cherubs. In this role, Satan had direct access to the throne of God.

For this reason, we know we are dealing with a powerful being in the spiritual realms. He is a force of destruction that comes from being an anointed angel who now has legions of followers who are fallen angelic beings, referred to as demons. These demons are also able to perform wonders. Satan counts on tantalizing and tickling your ears so you hear what you want to hear. This is especially true if you deal in the psychic arenas. Do not be deceived by the false belief that psychic hotlines are just for fun. Satan is the high priest of counterfeit. Jesus is the High Priest of truth. The only way to fully understand and not fall into a trap of copycat miracles is to fix your eyes on the one true God and be able to identify His love in your life. Understanding the origins of Anointed Cherub allows us to take him seriously and not accept the counterfeit miracles. Ladies, because it's natural to have a tendency to dwell on much of the past, and what Satan is doing, you must be encouraged to spend more time with the Lord. It is worth repeating: Satan is a defeated foe.

Lucifer

Satan's Trait: Lucifer is called the Morning Star before his fall from heaven. Now Lucifer presents himself as a counterfeit. He can come as an angel of light and seem to illuminate the path.

God's Truth: God's truth sets people free. He will never hide.

Lucifer is more than the cat's name in the story of Cinderella. In fact, the writers must have purposefully chosen that name because the cat in their story seemed sweet and nice, but was also able to pounce, scratch and create havoc.

The name Lucifer actually means Day Star or Morning Star. We read in Second Corinthians chapter 11 verse 14 that the enemy masquerades as an angel of light and a servant of righteousness. In Isaiah chapter 14 verse 12, we read reference to Satan as the morning star, son of the dawn who is cast down to earth. While light traditionally illuminates, he is counterfeit and we may fall into a trap of believing we have arrived unblemished and whole. Lucifer seeks to impart empty promises. However, things that go against God's plan may have captivated you without your realization. When we put truth in the light, we do not give Satan the opportunity to use it and counterfeit what God is doing in our lives.

We have the freedom to walk in true light through asking Jesus Christ to come into our hearts and be Lord of our lives. This truth cannot be counterfeit. Only with the Lord is there such true peace and light.

The god of this age

Satan's Trait: This false god has been around a very long time and has extensive knowledge of human behavior and patterns.

God's Truth: If you ask for divine wisdom, you may be surprised to have wisdom beyond your years to deal with this ancient enemy.

Growing up and understanding the African-American culture, I heard the saying about young people who seemed to have wisdom beyond their age or circumstance. These young people seem to have an "old soul." Today, we need "Old Soul" wisdom, because we are fighting an enemy who accumulates novels of understanding about the human condition.

In Second Corinthians chapter 4 verse 4 we read, "The god of this age had blinded the minds of both believers and unbelievers alike, so that they cannot see the light of the gospel of the glory of Christ, who is the image of God." This really answers the question why some people understand the freedom and joy of the Lord and others seem blind to the pure light of the gospel. It also enables us to purpose to seek wisdom and pray for those who do not know Jesus Christ as their savior as well as those believers who remain trapped in strongholds. It is apparent that the god of this age, Satan, can only be defeated in the spiritual level for people to come into a saving knowledge of Christ. Satan is not all that, as the young say. Make no mistake. He has knowledge; however, the Word gives us the wisdom to unveil him.

The Prince of this World

Satan's Trait: The enemy is able to roam this world and can communicate with God. The Prince will attempt to entice and control peoples' minds.

God's Truth: It is strategically possible to develop the ability to put on the full armor for victory in the battle.

In the Book of John chapter 12 verses 31 and 32, Jesus says judgment is upon this world; and the ruler of this world loses. Also, in the Book of Ephesians chapter 2 verses 1 and 2 it says "As for you, you were dead in your transgressions and sins, in which you used to live when you followed the ways of this world and the ruler of the kingdom of the air, the spirit who is now at work in those who are disobedient."

It is important to take captive the lies of the enemy. Satan will mess with your mind so much that it may seem you are going crazy at times. There are mind battles that the Prince of this world will throw out to cause people to question and second-guess themselves. When your thinking includes "should," "but" and "ought" in your head, check it with the truth you already know. God has given us the gift of a free will. Although with this gift comes great responsibility and the potential to choose wrong as well as correct pathways. Know, my sisters, there is always a U-turn granted by the Lord. Paul reminds us in Ephesians chapter six to be strong in our intimate relationship with the Lord. Paul encourages us to walk in the strength of the Lord and put on the full armor, so that we will be able to stand against the schemes of the enemy. When we seek forgiveness and link ourselves to the victory of Christ through relationship with Him, we are able to defeat the Prince of this world. We link wholeheartedly with the one true King of Kings.

The Serpent of Old

Satan's Trait: Satan is the same today as he was in the ancient days of old. He is still a serpent bent on deceiving and highlighting unmet needs.

God's Truth: God is always near and He will never leave nor forsake you. Jesus, who sits at the right hand of Father God, is your intercessor.

The Book of Revelations chapter 12 verse 9 uses the description of Satan as the Serpent of Old. When inner turmoil wells up in life and it is new to you, it is not new to the author of destruction. This enemy, The Serpent of Old is the same Serpent today as he was in the Garden of Eden. The only exception is he has had more practice honing his deceptive tactics to be more purposeful and powerful at creating inner turmoil based on unmet fleshly desires. His plans to entice humankind with personal desires are revealed in the Book of James chapter one verses 13 and 14.

Many people experience a feeling I call, "hole in the soul." People will attempt to fill a hole by meeting their desires. Even though the feelings may come from legitimate needs, the serpent plants illegitimate needs. They may try to fill the holes with counterfeit methods such as addictions or unhealthy relationships. If you have ever experienced this deception, then you know, the feeling temporarily subsides and often when it returns, the void seems bigger than before.

The Great Dragon

Satan's Trait: The temptation of the Great Dragon is a consuming fire, designed to crush or entrap.

God's Truth: God is able to bring beauty out of the ashes in all lives.

It is interesting how God speaks metaphorically in the Book of Revelation chapter 12 verses 7 to 9 where He refers to Satan as a dragon. The verses tell the story of Satan's removal from heaven. God tells us of the great dragon's plunge from Heaven – that ancient serpent called the devil, or Satan, takes a plunge to earth and his angels with him.

A dragon, defined as a large snake or serpent, is also described as a gigantic reptile having a lion's claw and the tail of a serpent with wings. The Great Dragon is the same as the serpent of Eden and he still tempts with food. He also uses shopping, gossip, business, prestige or anything he thinks will work. All addictions eventually destroy self-worth, identity, dignity, hope, faith, passions and dreams leading to despair and heartache,.

When you feel tempted by food, shopping, gambling, men or any desire, you must realize this is the same tactic faced by Eve. However, we have historical awareness of using our free will. Take note, even if dreams, hopes, or identity have gone up in smoke, be of good courage. God will take your ash remnant and resurrect a new dream. At the same time, God is a gentleman, so He will not cross your free will. When the dragon comes against you be prepared and armed. The weapon of faith will vanquish the tactics of the great dragon. We can choose to remind the great dragon that he is cast out of heaven and has no place in our lives. We choose to walk the path of our Lord. Take time out of your day and meditate on Hebrews 4:12. God will not allow the flames sent by the great dragon to consume us.

The Father of Lies

Satan's Trait: The Father of Lies uses an element of truth, which may be woven into a lie that people choose to act out.

God's Truth: God unshackles the chains of lies with His truth and permits us to walk in freedom.

Everyone who spent time on a grade school playground understands the pain of hearing your name, reputation or identity linked to a lie. When a person is a liar, they intentionally present falsehoods that create a false impression or image.

Adam and Eve heard the tempter's lies and then chose to act on the lie. Often, lies have an element of truth woven through them as a hook of deception. These hooks become a doorway to many false beliefs and lifestyle bondages. Satan is not the creator and he is not creative. The Book of John chapter 8 verse 44 describes Satan as not holding to the truth, for there is not truth in him. He uses what is already in each person and then capitalizes on their unhealed wounds, hardened bitter roots, generational patterns and ties with unhealthy people.

God has called Satan many things, but victor is not among them. However, God tells us if our identity is in Christ, we are more than conquerors. Understanding this information gives us power to defeat the enemy of our soul because we are able to identify him and not allow him power in our life. You have truth. Unrealistic willpower does not set us free, but rather we are free by the grace of God. Knowing the enemy, lends itself to a certain advantage of predictability. The enemy will take every opportunity to inform you of the areas of unmet needs and holes in your heart. Sometimes the vacancies in your heart fill with the false lies of the enemy. However, it is so sweet when a heart chooses forgiveness, release and the path of walking in the freedom of the future. We are princess warriors and God is the captain. He goes before us in battle. When we do the practical with God's anointed power, He will do the supernatural.

Chapter 3 *Unveiling the Enemy ~ Reflection*

1. In what ways have you seen the enemy attempt to steal truth from your life?

2. When you think of the names God calls Satan, what name matches how you see the enemy active in your past?

3. Do you understand you have great power by knowing the enemy's name and understanding there is more power in the name of Jesus Christ? How does that make you feel?

Journal Notes ~ Write your additional thoughts and how an understanding of the names of the enemy can help you defeat him by your identity in Jesus Christ.

Chapter 4
Tactics of the Enemy

"Your word is a lamp to my feet and a light for my path."*(Psalm 119:105)*

It was as if she could not wake herself from a bad dream. It seemed tears had permanently stained her pillowcase, although those around her at work would not have known. She felt as if she was suffocating from a mask pressed over her face. Looking in the mirror, she saw no mask. No one else would either, but she knew her face showed false expressions to remain acceptable during the day. However when she removed her mask of acceptability during private hours, she felt an inescapable void. At first there had been comfort wearing the mask of a huge smile and telling everyone she was fine. Now, it had become a habit and she didn't know if she would even recognize her true smile.

Then she remembered what she heard at a women's Bible study, she didn't have to fight for herself. She only needed to recognize herself as a daughter of God and take up her identity as His beautiful creation. She wasn't sure how to do it, but knew she must trust the Lord or she'd never really smile again. She stood straighter realizing that through Christ, she already had victory over her past and she began to identify the tactics used to try to keep her in a victim mentality. Yes, through Christ she could become more than a conqueror.

We can have continual victory with Jesus Christ over all the tactics of the enemy as we stand firm against his schemes. Victory is not the end-result of our life, but a result of Jesus' resurrection from the dead after persecution and death on the cross. It is because of Him defeating death that our chains of bondage are broken. He gives us the keys to unlock each link of a chain the enemy would try to use to bind us. We are set free to walk in victory. The truth has set you free.

Therefore, we can hold our heads high and walk in victory as we discover the tactics of the enemy who wages a war against all humanity. When we identify Satan's methods, we become stronger in our ability to stand in the battle and smile at the same time. We know we are on the winning team. Let's more closely examine the names God calls Satan. We will follow the order of the last chapter and now add a greater understanding of the specific tactics the enemy will try to use to defeat us. Remember, ladies, we can examine this with full victory as if reading the enemy's battle plans and knowing how to defeat him at his own game.

Tactics of the "Adversary"

Why is it, when we are feeling ill, tired or overwhelmed, something else seems to come along that just seems too much to bear? Remember, the Adversary prowls around like a lion looking for those he can devour. When a lion hunts, he looks for a weak, vulnerable, isolated, inexperienced, young and unprotected animal. He wants to devour, not simply maim his prey, and he will use whatever means necessary.

Understand this: we are fighting an enemy who is not capable of grace or mercy. If you are around people who allow Satan to rule their life, you may often feel like you become the prey. There is a powerless feeling attributed to the relationships with certain people. It leaves you nearly stunned and thinking about what just happened because it doesn't always make sense. If this is the case, you may have just experienced a "Grace Killer." Sometimes, you know the experience, but cannot quite identify the reason.

Grace Killers are people who attack, shame, neglect, or reject everyone around them. Some Grace Killers refuse to see the changes in behavior you have made to grow. They do not let you forget how you used to act. Do you remember how you felt after being in the presence of a Grace Killer? It can feel like something has ripped your insides apart and rendered you exposed and powerless.

The hurt can be overwhelming. This powerless feeling robs hope, peace, confidence and security. Women have shared they felt like a whirlwind hit and were left asking, "What tornado just damaged my heart?" Grace Killers leave a person feeling an awful emptiness. This, my sisters, is the Adversary's goal. He wants to leave you torn apart, feeling empty and devoured in a river of never-ending hopelessness.

If the Adversary has used a person you live or work with, you may be groping for answers to questions such as: "Why do I continue to gravitate to the same destructive cycles?" You may have men in your life that seems to be great at first and then becomes controlling and manipulative and may leave you feeling powerless. However, when you evaluate your patterns and choices, it hits you like a ton of bricks! These people may have different names, but possess the same grace killing characteristics.

If you fall prey to the lion instincts of Satan the Adversary, you may start thinking like a victim. You may say something like, "How could I let myself be blind- sided again?" I want to encourage you to realize the fight is not in the flesh, but the principalities of the air. Frequently, a person who has been beaten down due to life's perils will feel abandoned by others and even God. Satan the Adversary laughs at this emotion of abandonment. He counts on you dwelling in that emotion and entertaining ways you can alleviate the pain. The adversarial enemy will agitate you and create all manner of frustration. Satan does not care if you are down. He does not care if you are bleeding. He wants you wiped out. He does not want you to be recovered, restored or transformed. However, this isn't the end of the story because in the book of John chapter 10, verse 10 Jesus tells us He has come so we would have life and have it to the fullest. God wants you to live a life of peace and joy. The power of words can decrease or increase joy. It is possible to speak life or death to your own spirit. We know this because the book of Proverbs tells us that out of the heart the mouth speaks.

Broken relationships can shatter trust and result in tortured souls. Addictions and unhealthy substitutes can unfortunately replace true intimacy and create a false lens of reality. To cope with life, people may begin to create the reality they want others to see. Yet, the false environment keeps them from the real connections and intimacy they ulti- mately desire. The longing to be loved, valued and affirmed becomes lost in the mire of unrealistic and false perceptions of self, others and God. Change is not a simple process, but Sisters it is worth the journey. Life is not single layered, so the journey of transformation also has many layers to peel through and determine the truth of the real you. This means change involves a deeper look at the shadows you may have taken on as truth. You must sift through to uncover the true you. It's time to get real about the good, bad and the ugly in life and choose to be set free. Getting things out in the open exposes them to light, before Satan's darkness can influence truth. The enemy uses spiritual struggles in our thoughts, emotions and will. The Adversary knows these struggles are in proportion to the release of your faith. The enemy wants to weaken your faith and prevent you from receiving the promises of your Abba Father. When you take responsibility for your actions, Satan has no power in the situation.

Remember, we must confront the lies of the enemy and replace it with a truth or promise from the Word of God. We have to be on guard because the Adversary is an opponent with no capacity to show mercy. However, we can claim that our identity is not determined by our past, but, rather, in whom God says we are. Standing in the battle often involves confronting our choices in relationships. If you notice the identity of Grace Killers in your life, there is a path to take that leads to freedom from the Adversary using Grace Killers to keep you from the true you. I recommend you pull out your journal and write each step you take so you are able to untangle your thoughts and see God's truth revealed. This will also give you a place to return and read your journey to see the growth and multiple layers you uncover.

Here are the stepping-stones to stay on a healthy path to freedom.

- *Pray.* Ask the Lord for help with facing life realities. Allow the Lord to open your heart and receive His love and truth.

- *Admit it.* If you are hurt, disappointed and fearful, do not minimize those feelings and their impact on your life. Take time to do the process of healing from a painful past.

- *Confess to God.* Since He already knows, it's a good time to fess up to God and even possibly to a safe person. You can confess to take responsibility and you can admit how you feel about different actions and events that have influenced your life.

- *Renew your mind.* Reading God's Living Word, the Bible, will bring power and truth to your thoughts. You must recognize that it takes the Lord's strength to receive hope, courage and boldness.

- *Step into forgiveness.* Like this journey, forgiveness is not a single step, but many stepping stones on the path to health. Do not abandon the process of grief which will include forgiving yourself, others and God. Often, forgiveness is also an act of obedience to God because you may have to do it before you feel like it. Do not wait until you feel the feeling to forgive. Often emotions follow actions.

- *Exchange your plan for God's plan.* Remember, if you choose to change nothing, then it is certain nothing will change. Even if you are on the right road, and you stand there without taking action, it is a guarantee you will be unchanged.

- *Prepare for practice.* Anytime you step into new behaviors, it takes practice and you must be ready for internal resistance. When anyone takes new steps, it is very easy to question the new course. You have to resist the temptation to second-guess this new healthy behavior. Avoid statements that involve "I shouldn't have," and be enthusiastic about your new healthy boundaries. The enemy will attempt to make you feel it is better to go back to previous familiar thinking or ways. You may experience external resistance from well-meaning people because they were comfortable with the way things were. However, if you are patient with yourself and do not give up on the journey, you are guaranteed by God that you will walk into new freedom.

It is time to grab onto the freedom because you know the truth: Satan lost and God won! Between life and death, there is God's story, our story and Satan's story. Scripture says we are to run with endurance and persistence the race set before us. When we look towards Jesus, who is the author and finisher of our faith, we can run the race. At the end of the journey, the question is about how we ran our race. If we ran well, it means we chose to run the direction God had planned when He chose the racecourse. The truth we must embrace is if we confess and humble ourselves, Satan has nothing to work with because there is nothing God cannot redeem. If we are followers of Jesus Christ, we will go to our heavenly home at our death where our true inheritance will be unveiled. We cannot lose if we choose to embrace the truth. Those who God sets free are free indeed. As you journal, refer back to these truths as your light along the path to standing in the battle.

Tactics of the "Slanderer"

The Slanderer's goal is to create a place of doubt concerning your identity in Christ. He wants you to reject God. This is why when you step in a new direction, or face challenges, you may doubt your own abilities. You may even seem to hear the teasing of your youth rather than the teaching of wisdom. Remember, the Slanderer imparts false assumptions, fear of rejection, abandonment or triggers of negative experiences creating a war within your own soul. When we choose to heal, we create opportunities for God to set us free. I call these new opportunities "art experiences" because they are openings for God to draw upon a new canvas. Unfortunately, people find it difficult to lay down negative life experiences. A trigger will take a person back to the event and resurrect the same emotional experience. The way we perceive and give meaning to negative experiences is often more important than the original event. Nevertheless, if we learn to heal from past pain by practicing healthy responses to painful triggers, we can choose to allow God to work on new canvas. We have a choice to let the past triggers control us and allow our mind to become Satan's playground or we can battle to defeat the enemy and live as a new canvas for the Lord to create great victories in the battle.

Making the choice to get to the real you involves replacing all destructive self-talk with renewed thinking. This is integral in the ability to make healthy choices and not remain stuck in the muck. For example, if you have ever been shamed, the natural tendency is to set up protective mechanisms, such as putting on masks to prevent further hurt. Exposing the reason you took on a mask in the first place is essential to removing the mask and getting to the real you. Because masks serve to cloak, protect, hide or costume you, living life without a mask takes some getting use to. However, it's worth it when you don't have to sort the masks and can just wake-up fresh and ready for a day of walking with God as He intends you to be.

I want to identify six main masks women wear so you can take an inventory of your personal decisions:

- *The Mask of Independence* — Women who wear this mask have faced repeated rejection, hurt and emotional abandonment. Eventually, an inner message emerges which states, "I don't need anybody."

- *The Mask of Compliance* — Women who have faced physical, emotional, verbal, spiritual or sexual abuse wear this mask. Through the abuse, these women experience a stripping away of their personal value. It is imperative they not abandon the process of grief, which will include the kind of forgiveness referred to previously. The inner message which emerges is, "I'll be whatever you want me to be to prevent further abuse."

- *The Mask of Dependency* — Women who wear this mask have faced extreme abandonment and have lost the will to fight for themselves. Because they begin to believe they aren't worthy and function through a victim mindset, they develop dependence in relationships. The inner message is "As long as you take care of me, I will be whatever you want."

- *The Mask of Achievement* — Women who wear this mask have faced criticism and begun to believe they are never good enough. Because of this perfectionism, they perform to obtain personal validation. The inner message playing is, "I'll work harder and harder and then you will love and accept me."

- *The Mask of Change* – Women who wear this chameleon-like mask have faced the pressure of other peoples' opinions. To find acceptance, significance, security and love, these women have laid down their uniqueness in order to adapt to fit various situations. They lose their true self and an inner message says, "I'll become what people think I am."

- *The Mask of Make-Believe* — Women who wear this pretending-like mask have faced betrayal from those they allowed to get close. Because it's risky for them to allow their real personality to emerge, they don't allow anyone to become emotionally close. Their inner message becomes, "I can never trust anyone again, so I won't depend on others."

The method of putting on masks can eventually turn into walls around your heart. The protective masks not only keep bad things out; it also prevents good from entering. Additionally, people will make internal vows to prevent further injury. Have you ever made a promise to yourself that goes something like this? "I will never let anyone get too close to me again. They only want to take advantage of me." If you have made any similar vows, today is a day of victory as you identify this tactic of the Slanderer. The enemy wants to rob you from the joy of God's ultimate love in your life. You are not alone. A wonderful spiritual warfare tool is finding a relationship where you are accountable, which breaks the isolation. Safe accountability partners will speak truth with love. They help to bring issues into the light. The enemy hates when women choose to live in the light of truth.

Women, who have learned to accept the love of Jesus but find it extremely painful to be vulnerable and trust Father God, will also be a target for the enemy to employ his battle tactics. This lack of intimacy and trust with your creator stems from a variety of root issues and repeated personal hurts. By understanding the origins of those issues, and claiming identity in Christ, the right relationship with Father God can be re-established.

Earthly parenting is vital in how children and adults accept their heavenly Father. Consider, for example, the parents who are emotionally distant from their own children. If this happens long-term, a child may grow up to view God as being personally disinterested in their life. There will be distance in this spiritual relationship. It is vital you understand how this may give the Slanderer a foothold. People may take on an identity as a victim or become deceived and seek comfort in things such as food, shopping, relationships, and even ministry rather than taking refuge with God.

The key to unlocking freedom from the Slanderer is to release the repetitive negative talk of the past. Self-talk is a powerful tape that can play in a person's mind. You may be doing fine and come across an old photograph or trigger a memory that turns on that tape of negative thinking. If you are not in a healthy relationship with God or others, you may let the tape play and run with the lies and distortions. When this happens, the Slanderer tries to claim victory by causing you to doubt yourself, others and ultimately God. This produces a false guilt and isolation from God. It also stops you from taking ownership for your choices. The Slanderer is a master at twisting things to make you blame someone else for the consequences of your free will.

Satan has used this battle tactic since the beginning of time. As you remember, after being deceived and choosing to eat of the fruit, Adam's first statement to God was, "You gave this woman to me and she gave me the forbidden fruit." It is really the original example of shifting blame. He blamed Eve and God for his choice. Next, Eve blamed the serpent.

When someone cannot connect with their identity to Father God, or feel God is not fully giving them their due, they begin to doubt. The Slanderer would have us doubt everything, shift blame and create an inner turmoil, which says, "I must take control."

Really, we can return to the truth originally mentioned and develop our identity with God by looking to Psalm 139 and realizing God knit us together with His own hand. We are fearfully and wonderfully made. We have victory and can hold our heads high knowing we have a purpose from the beginning and that is worth standing in the battle.

Tactics of "Abaddon" ~ author of destruction

Have you ever been hurting so bad you do not know if you can pray? You try to read the Bible and it no longer seems to hold any promises for you. The pain may make you feel numb. Decisions may not be clear. If you relate to this, you are in a valley place, but you still have power in the truth of God's Word. You have tools that you may not understand. It would be a mistake to stop reading the Bible and praying.

When the Bible does not seem to make sense or resonate with your life and you do not really know what you are reading, it may be even more important to read the Word. You will gain clarity as you navigate the valley and even if you do not know what you are reading, the Word is a living Word and it will never return void.

Remember, the Holy Spirit will interpret for us and Jesus stands at the right hand of Father God interceding on our behalf. He literally stands in the gap praying for us. Jesus interprets our very tears to the Heavenly Father.

Abaddon is a name God uses when dealing with the enemy who desires to crush us. The name means destruction. If we are dealing with Satan and he tries this tactic, we may feel like a bomb has gone off in our life and we feel crushed. Our hopes may have faded and we are discouraged. In that discouragement, we may even feel embarrassed and weak. Abaddon will try to claim victory.

However, if we can acknowledge and expose our own weakness to people who will understand, we will be walking in victory. The light floods our lives when we walk with truth, even if we are feeling defeated. Truth still prevails because what Abaddon would use to produce shame, confusion and bondage, will turn to allow others into your life. When we practice open accountability with people who value a relationship with God, the result will be honest relationships, assistance and love. When we experience God's light, darkness cannot prevail. We can cry out to God for right relationships and rebuilding of what Satan seemingly destroyed.

Abaddon knows the power we have when we cry out to God in Jesus' name. Our enemy understands the power of prayer. We must utilize the power of prayer and declare the power of God's promises as we earnestly seek Him to intervene in our lives. Remember, you have a destiny beyond yourself and you have forgiveness for the mistakes of the past as you walk into new battlegrounds in victory.

Tactics of "Beelzebub" ~ lord of the flies

When something bad from the past creeps into your mind, do you experience it just as if it were yesterday? Is a relationship with someone who is not even walking the earth any longer still lingering with painful memories in your mind? It is time to clear away the dead things to walk in freedom and not allow Beelzebub any area of entry to feed off the dead of our past. We walk as new creations through Christ Jesus.

We must know the truth in order to confront distorted belief systems built into our lives. Beelzebub uses distorted thinking to threaten God's plan for individuals, churches and even godly corporations.

To confront the enemy's tactic, we must separate lies from the truth. Whether the events of life are perceived or real, we can replace them with wisdom and seek personal freedom. It may be difficult, but begin reading the Book of Proverbs. It is better than a one-a-day multivitamin. You can read one Proverb a day for a month and have taken in the entire book of wisdom. The next month, read it again and begin to build on the wisdom by applying the principles. Reading it repeatedly will bring a continual wash of wisdom like refreshing waves cleansing your perceptions.

Beelzebub would like to claim victory by keeping you shackled in chains, even though the jail doors are open. It is up to you to walk through any needed grief process, accept wisdom, lay down lies and break free from past pain.

Grief is an individual journey and appears in a variety of forms. To become an over-comer, we must learn to live in our new skin and create revised thought patterns. We must be quickly able to identify triggers, which attempt to set a course of unhealthy behaviors or thinking.

Many women choose to sit down on the journey still wearing a victim robe. Often they come close to freedom and then pull back just when a break through may be around the next bend. God desires we live in this broken and fallen world as victorious women standing tall in the battle and cloaked in His glory.

Remember, you have a destiny beyond yourself and the mistakes of the past. You can stand forgiven and begin to walk into new battleground.

Tactics of the "Anointed Cherub"

Have you ever experienced what you thought was an answer to prayer, only to question later if the consequences of it could possibly be in God's plan for you? You are not alone if the challenges of answered horoscopes and strange coincidence that have you shaking your head and wondering how much power Satan really has. The answers are in the book of Ezekiel where we see the enemy has a lot of power. In fact, we must have the Lord's help in discerning it because we see that Satan actually has the power to imitate God.

Sister, it is not time to stop reading and be downcast. When we really understand this, we know we are on the winning team. Let us look further at the Anointed Cherub that covers. The Bible tells us he was, and is, an anointed but fallen spirited angel and therefore, he has no flesh and blood limitations. This is a mysterious point that had me shaking my head for a time. God did not only give Satan authority, but God also limited him. This is a powerful revelation. We are dealing with a powerful being in the spiritual realms. It will take supernatural powers to fight the enemy of God.

Now we know why psychic hotlines work. They work to deceive because the force behind them is evil and comes from an anointed angel and demons, which are able to perform wonders and seeming miracles. Satan counts on tantalizing and tickling our ears so we hear what we desire to hear. The Anointed Cherub is really the high priest of counterfeit. In Second Corinthians chapter 11 verse 14, we see that he has adapted through the years to make himself look like one of the good people. Like a chameleon, he can become any color he needs in order to deceive.

However, even though the horoscopes come daily in the newspaper to deceive, we can trust daily in the Living Word from our Father God. In fact, when we read the Bible, we are quickly reassured that the enemy is already defeated. The Anointed Cherub is still only a created being. He is not Elohim, the Creator, who is the source of freedom. Remember, by understanding the origins of the Anointed Cherub we can take him seriously and not accept his counterfeit miracles. When you know the real thing, you will discern truth. It is like counterfeit money; it only has value if the one receiving it cannot discern it from the real thing.

Tactics of "Lucifer"

Have you ever kept doing something you thought might be wrong, but also thought it probably wasn't hurting anything? Maybe you held to a behavior that you suspected didn't please God, but also thought it was no big deal. Do you have any hidden habits? It is time to take hold of what is really happening when God calls Satan Lucifer, the deceiver of our soul. Lucifer has a goal to capture God's children and have us believe we are fine even when we are in sin.

When Lucifer uses this tactic, we have power by choosing to get well. If we choose to seek wisdom and overcome deception, we begin to mature in ways that allow us to choose the path of freedom. We develop the habit of choosing the better thing. We choose what is holy rather than what may be easy. When we claim victory and call on the name of God, He is faithful to release all we need. If you need wisdom, you can ask God to grow you. Just as King Solomon asked for wisdom, you can ask to become wise and overcome deception.

Remember, Lucifer the deceiver wouldn't make it so easy by appearing in a red tail and horns, however, he is the master of counterfeit and can come as an angel of light and seem to illuminate our path. As you pray for wisdom, you will choose the real light and seek God's plans for your life.

Tactics of "the god of the age"

Have you ever wondered why the pop culture atmosphere can make you downcast? You show up to a place wearing chunky heel shoes only to find stilettos are back in style. If this affects your mood, your ability to step in confidence may cause you to miss opportunities in sharing Christ with others. You may be dealing with the "god of the age."

When cultural norms and tasks of the day make us feel defeated, we may derail from the plan God has for us. That is when "the god of the age" senses his own victory. He has volumes of historical information on humanity, whereas we have only our lifetime of knowledge and that which we have studied of recorded history. Therefore, we must realize the potential power of his use of pop culture, his understanding of human emotion and his desire to derail us from our destiny.

We have victory over "the god of the age" when we know who we are in Christ and claim our identity as daughters of the Almighty God. That perspective makes our shoe style matter less and where we walk matter more. In the book of Ephesians chapter one verse 13 we read, "Blessed be the God and Father of our Lord Jesus Christ, who has blessed us with every spiritual blessing in the heavenly places in Christ."

Remember, through our identity in Christ as daughters of the King, our ability to pray and our desire to read the Bible, we will enjoy wisdom beyond our years and have victory over an ancient enemy.

Tactics of the "Prince of this World"

Have you ever felt as if weariness in the battle would overtake you? Sometimes it is not even the magnitude of the challenge, but the length of the journey that creates daily weariness. That is when the "Prince of this World" or "Ruler of the Kingdom of the Air" desires to overtake you. The enemy would have you so tired and wounded in the battle of daily living that you could even blame God for your life circumstance. The enemy knows if the drudgery of life gets you down, you could turn on God and confuse the enemy attacks with God not caring about your circumstances.

We read in the book of Job about the enemy tactics of total ruin and even friends who misinterpreted Job's devotion and love of God. They told Job he must have done something wrong for God to let all this bad stuff happen. They began to shift blame from the enemy battle to a battle with the Lord.

To achieve victory over this enemy we must fight battle fatigue by seeking a stronger relationship with Father God and our own ability to persevere will expand. That is where our eternal victory is measured. God is a Redeemer; however, He respects the free will we possess. We can choose the things of God and be strong in the daily battles. Paul tells us in Ephesians chapter six beginning in verse 10 to "Be strong in the Lord and in the strength of His might. Put on the full armor of God, so that you will be able to stand firm against the schemes of the devil."

Knowing this, we can put on our spiritual armor and continue in the daily battles without weariness. The enemy is like an arms dealer waiting to try new weapons. When we know this and the battle seems too tough, we must remember the war is the Lord's and He knows every weapon and how much of the battle we can handle. Sometimes we may think God has more faith in our ability to fight and develop character than we have faith in His ability to know what we can handle.

Our personal battle may be physical, behavioral, emotional or psychological. Any of these may be an entry point for the enemy to rage a battle for our soul. However, we are to be proactive rather than reactive. We can choose daily to respond and take up the spiritual armor, which we discuss in detail in chapter seven. When we respond with the tools God gives us rather than react in our circumstances, we are really standing firm in the battle.

Remember, God has allowed the enemy the freedom to roam, just as we have the freedom to choose and strategically develop our spiritual abilities to stand victoriously in the battle.

Tactics of the "Great Dragon"

Have you ever felt as if your hopes and dreams went up in a puff of smoke and all you have left are the charred remains of what you thought life would be at this point? If so, you may have wrestled with Satan as the Great Dragon.

When children play with small plastic figures of dragons, they often pretend the dragon is a fire-breathing monster who burns the drawbridge and enters the kingdom to get the princess. Really, the Great Dragon is much like the toys in that the creature consumes until there is nothing left after the consuming fire. He is the same serpent as the creature that tempted Eve in the garden. Only now, he is bent on heating things up for you until you are consumed and your dreams are gone. On the other hand, you may feel like things are heating up so fast and the enemy can count on you reaching burnout. Either way he attempts to claim victory by robbing you of your God-given destiny.

To stand in victory, read about Esther in the Bible and how the Lord created beauty from the ashes. Also in the book of Joel, chapter two, we see that God is the Redeemer and He is able to restore what the locust eats.

Remember, the Great Dragon may be the same as the serpent of Eden and will try to consume your dreams, but you have the power to defeat him by using your free will to choose to pursue your destiny regardless of circumstance.

Tactics of the Father of Lies

Have you ever heard the first person's version of a story and gotten angry for them, only to hear the second and realize they pulled you into a lie? When a false impression or purposely-deceptive image presents, the Father of Lies is involved.

The enemy tactic is to create a doorway and seed unresolved turmoil. As was earlier stated, the Father of Lies is not the creator and is not creative. However, he will stir things up to capitalize on conflict. It is his tactic to use those unhealed areas of our life, the bitter roots, generational curses and ties with unhealthy people to pull us into a deceptive cycle.

The Father of Lies attempts to trigger our bad memories with snapshots of the past that would remind us of areas of unforgiveness, bitterness or damage. If he gets us to linger in that stinking thinking, he will have energized a deceptive cycle and try to claim victory.

The Father of Lies revels in the idea that we try to be our own god by being self-sufficient and taking control of everything. We may even try to play god for others. When women fall into this trap, they become like an experiment of adaptability. When room temperature water placed in bowl sits on a hot plate, a frog will remain in it with a fair amount of comfort. As the water temperature slowly increases by 10 degrees over a 10-minute timeframe, the frog remains in the water. He is a healthy frog with the complete ability to jump from the bowl of water. Although there are not physical barriers to jumping, the frog remains in the water. It adapts to each temperature increase because he is unfamiliar with what is outside the bowl. The frog remains in the water even to death, because while he is miserable, he is also in a familiar environment.

In dealing with the Father of Lies, we must not always try to adapt to our circumstances and control everything. We must jump even when it seems uncomfortable so we can move away from unhealthy behaviors or relationships. If the Father of Lies claims victory, we will stay with what is killing us and continue to adapt until it just feels normal to do so.

We claim victory over the Father of Lies by trusting in the grace of God that sets us free. It is a lot better than unrealistic willpower that continually leads to failure. Every time the Father of Lies reminds you of your past, you must remind him of his eminent defeat. You can remind Satan of his loss based on the predestined victory described throughout the Bible.

Remember, while there may be an element of truths woven into a lie, you are able to know the full truth, confront the lie and stand strong in the battle to defeat the Father of Lies. God tells us in the book of James Chapter 1 to ask for wisdom. Knowledge is awesome, but wisdom gives us the divine insight into the timing of the Lord.

Congratulations! You now have a tremendous understanding of the names God calls our enemy and the tactics the enemy will employ in an attempt to reach his goal of defeating your destiny. You also have the saving knowledge of Jesus Christ interceding on your behalf at the right hand of Father God. Additionally, we know because through the resurrection of Jesus Christ, we already have victory and the enemy cannot resurrect sin from the past because you receive forgiveness the moment you ask through the blood of Christ.

As daughters of your Heavenly Father, you can hold your head high and take a stand in the battle waging around you. You can stand victorious as you continue your journey. Next, we will use our understanding to better apprehend God's plan for us through His redemptive power.

Chapter 4 *Tactics of the Enemy ~ Reflection*

1. In what ways have you identified the enemy's tactics in your life?

2. When you think of the tactics the enemy most often tries in your life, what can you do to improve your personal response?

3. Do you understand you can defeat the enemy through daily time with the Lord by reading the Bible and praying simple prayers?

Journal Notes ~ Write your additional thoughts and how your understanding of the tactics of the enemy can help you defeat him simply by developing a battle plan.

Part II

TAKING A STAND IN THE SPIRITUAL BATTLE

Chapter 5

God's Redemptive Power

"Do not let this Book of the Law depart from your mouth; meditate on it day and night, so that you may be careful to do everything written in it. Then you will be prosperous and successful." *(Joshua 1:8, NIV)*

All she wanted was success and prosperity. She worked from early morning into the night and when it seemed ends didn't meet, she would take on another job. She was truly a worn-out woman. It seems her friends had the great jobs, great cars, great clothes and that is what she wanted. Before going into her next job, she rested her head on the steering wheel of her well-worn car. What was steering her? When would it be her turn for the great things she only dreamed?

Her eyes rested on the other cars in the lot. Not much different from her own, yet one with a Christian fish decal seemed to stand out. She knew it belonged to one of the nicest women at her work. They appeared to have the same job, yet this woman boldly professed even from her car sticker that she was a Christian. Yes, her prosperity and success came from the Greatness of God, rather than the great things she possessed. Before opening the car door, she made a decision to make today different from every other day. She would seek out the owner of the car and find out what made her so loving, peaceful, joyful, kind and great.

We make our plans, prepare our path, write our lists and pack our cars before heading out for any road trip. Along the way, things happen and our plans may change or we take turns we didn't expect. We may even have left items off our original list and have completely forgotten something so important to our journey. There may even be times when we pack our car so tight that we have no room for a friend to join us.

There is a better way when it comes to living our lives. This will be a long journey and we are always preparing for the next turn in the road. We may need to unpack some of our past baggage to make room for new attire. Remember, God looks at the intent of your hearts and not your weakness and failures. The enemy wants you to dwell in the land of defeat. Sisters, it is time to put on your new attire. Our new attire will include robes of righteousness and crowns of glory that are greater than anything we can work to purchase. The love of God will release His righteousness in your life.

At some point, you may feel like you have taken your own journey to the edge of a cliff and can only see the other side in the foggy distance. God is here to build the bridge and take you where you need to go. It is time for new territory on the map only He provides. Psalm chapter 34 verse 19 tells us "Many are the afflictions of the righteous; but the Lord delivers them out of them all."

When you apprehend God's plans for your journey and realize He has the ultimate map, you will be able to better relax and enjoy the view. Yes, the enemy will try to put roadblocks and speed bumps in your path to slow you down and make you change course, but God is involved and He will turn you around if you let Him.

No matter how your journey began, God has a plan. Your parents may not be ideal or even around. You may feel illegitimate by the world's standard, but in God's book, you are fully legitimate and He has a plan for you.

Begin today to boldly take hold of God's redemptive power by speaking to God and ask Him to turn around your situation. You may think there is a provision problem and you don't have all you need to repair your situation. However, God says there is no provision problem; instead, there is a revelation problem. In fact, God will interrupt your life and change your course when you ask for greater understanding. You will get a revelation about how God really sees you and the plans He has for your ultimate success.

When we redefine success to line up with God's view of success, we will experience greater contentment and joy. God wants to grow personal character and refine relationships. It is time for a change. Repeating the same behavior and expecting different results would be foolish. Sisters, we can change the road we're on by allowing God to be our bridge, our refuge, our strong tower, our battle-ax and our hiding place. In the Bible, the book of Genesis chapter 12 tells us to lift our eyes up. God will reposition you and release you to be about His business. People will be looking to you to see success when the Lord is magnified in your life.

In the first chapter of the book of Joshua in the Bible, we see that it is essential we speak the Word of God for full activation in our lives. God promises He will reveal Himself strong in the midst of any storm. God will increase authority and anointing to enlarge our influence. In Psalms chapter eight verse 11 and Exodus chapter 3 verses, nine through 20 we see that God is a God of super miracles. These miracles last over time and cannot be counterfeited by the enemy.

Over the years, I have worked with people who seem to walk in God's favor. I have also experienced God's favor. Sisters, it is easier than we make it. To walk in God's favor is to say, "Yes, Lord." As you say yes to His way and His will, favor follows. Favor is the ability to move in obedience to the call of God. We have received revelation about many things. Revelation is really just a key we receive. Favor comes when we use the key to begin opening doors and moving where we are directed by the Lord. Favor is when God releases wisdom and insight, which your original map wouldn't have provided. It is when someone receives power, truth and vision. Favor is revelation coming-to-pass and you moving in the direction that leads to even more blessing. Favor flows your way when you walk the walk and not simply talk the talk.

When we speak the Word of the Lord and move in the revelation we have received we are able to go just the right speed, at the right time, with the right direction and we are not the ones who have laid the journey. This is the beauty of God protecting the vision. He gives the path and becomes the driver of our course. Yet, God also delights in seeing people use their spiritual gifts, talents and abilities given to bring about the visions and dreams.

In the process of apprehending God's plans, we realize there is a season for everything under the sun. The wise women are those who do not miss the season. If you press into the Word, you will hear what you need when the time comes for you to move. You will also know if you are to press forward and forget the former things. Additionally, you will have discernment of areas where you must learn from things of your past. It is time to believe and understand that God will deliver you from the former things. The Word of God, the Bible, enables us to face seemingly impossible situations.

The favor of God may feel like it is undeserved. We cannot receive favor by being good enough all the time. We can, however, ask for favor and seek wisdom on our journey. Remember, we are God's daughters and no matter how we may have blown it, He loves His daughters. We are able to reach up to our Abba Father, ask for His deliverance of feeling unworthy, and receive the blessings. We do not have to pretend to have it all together. God uses ordinary people to accomplish extraordinary things.

God's plan is not for us to go alone on our journey. It is no surprise that today's churches are seventy percent women. God has a big heart for women and He purposely created her with a softness of heart to move for His people. He also knows women can have the strength of character to stand for faith, goodness and mercy. Often, when people first receive an understanding of God's love and ask the Lord into their hearts, it is because of a woman's prayer. They recount how a mother, grandmother, sister or an auntie had believed in and prayed for them.

Ladies, our call is to be in this world, speak God's Word, apprehend and activate His plans for us. We must tell others what God is doing in our lives and we need to keep believing in all the power of the Lord. In my youth, we called this type of sharing, "bearing witness to what The Lord our Savior had done in our lives." God is the one who began a good work in us and He will complete it until the day of Christ's return. We must claim our friends and families for God's purposes.

That said, you may look over the top of these pages and see someone who needs God's plan. They may be a stranger at the airport or someone across your living room. You know they need God's love, but it seems better in the book than in action. Well, Sisters, you are not alone. It can be scary to keep living with God's plans in mind. At some point when you have walked in God's favor long enough, it is scarier to think of living without God's plan than it is to take the risk of sharing His love with those around you.

Our faith must be bigger than our fear. We are part of something so much bigger than today. Your choices affect generations. When you walk with God's favor, others are drawn to you and your life reflects God's glory. Yes, this is possible. When you step out in the midst of fear, your faith becomes active. Ask the Lord to empower you to overcome fear.

The first step to living so people see the glory of God is to let down defense mechanisms and be yourself. When you seek God's face and receive full grace, you develop intimacy with the Lord. The Lord will give you the desires of your heart and you will develop an increased servant-heart for this world. It is an amazing process to lay down personal desires and agree with the will of the Lord. This in no way implies lying down and being a doormat to others unhealthy patterns and behaviors. However, it may mean doing mundane things such as picking up our family's socks instead of nagging them about getting them in the laundry. The beauty is others will often begin to do the very things we desired for them to do. We may find it is uncomfortable at first, but we begin to prefer the pursuit of agape love; in the process, the Lord adds favor to our lives.

Really, we begin to walk with excellence focused on others. It does not mean we become perfectionists, but we do strive for excellence. Excellence is the humble woman, who then becomes a steward of the things of God for the kingdom's sake. This is the result of a process of restoration. We lay down the things of the past and receive restoration along the way while stepping into the future.

One client came to me with a downcast soul, and her face was full of sadness and guilt. She wrapped up her story of challenges with a statement I have since heard repeated at women's conferences around the globe. "I just don't feel like I measure up." Her voice would crack as she told of attending church to seek God's freedom, only to walk out the doors and feel life press back in on her. She would see others who walk in God's favor and would crave their victory. Later she would emotionally spin out of control feeling bad that she was not happy for their successes.

The picture was clear. She was missing an understanding of the process of sanctification. Throughout our time, I was able to share a picture with her that you must also visualize. The truth that set her free was the concept that sanctification is about a process of growing. She needed to know she did not have to be perfect. Think of sanctification as the process from salvation to physical death. In the journey process of sanctification, there are hills, valleys, mountaintops and thorns along the trail. Each area involves character building, which is more important to the Lord than comfort. When we are half-way up the hill, the view is different from when we reach the mountaintop. While the mountaintop is beautiful, it is only a small part of the journey and we must keep moving to see the next success. The valleys may be difficult, but they can also be a time when we prepare for the push up the hill. We must press through the thorns to receive the sweetness of the berries or enjoy the aroma of the flowers.

This character-building picture is an analogy for life as we move through the sanctification process. There is freedom knowing we do not have to measure up to the world's standards. Living an excellent life, by God's standard, is our calling. The view may be different depending where we are in the sanctification process. The beauty of the journey is that we are becoming more Christ-like as we press through.

The woman, who came to my office downcast, feeling she could not measure up, now understands the full measure of God. She found comfort in one of my favorite songs that says, "If you can use anything, Lord, use me. Take my hands Lord and my feet, take my heart, Lord, and speak to me. If you can use anything, Lord, use me."

Now, when the Lord chooses to use us and we have apprehended God's plans, we are going to recognize what I call "Holy Assignments." We must be prepared to be uncomfortable and expect the unexpected. When you least plan for it, you will have a holy assignment to help someone in a parking lot, grocery story, neighborhood or anywhere you are. If you are available for God to use, He will make sure you are on the path of someone else who needs understanding, value or a cup of cold water on a hot day. Ask the Lord to bring you into a place of fresh anointing as you walk in your "Holy Assignments." God's favor goes beyond the symbol of the Christian fish on the back of a car, but He will use anything to gain our attention and lead us in holy assignments so we will continue to stand in the battle.

Chapter 5 *God's Redemptive Power ~ Reflection*

1. In what ways have you been mapping out your own life?

2. When you think of the mistakes and choices of the past, how has God redeemed them and how could He use them to add favor to your life now? What can you do to allow God to show you a new map for your life?

3. Do you understand you can overcome the enemy's roadblocks and apprehend God's plans for you by daily reading the Word of God and having regular conversations with Him?

Journal Notes ~ Write your additional thoughts and how your understanding of God's redemptive power can bring add power to your life and allow you to stand strong in the battle.

Chapter 6

Call on the Names of God

"For there is no difference between Jew and Gentile – the same Lord is Lord of all and richly blesses all who call on Him, for, "Everyone who calls on the name of the Lord will be saved." *(Romans 10:12, NIV)*

She reached for the phone, knowing it would only be busy again. Still she had to try. She needed answers. She needed someone to help her sort out her feelings, thoughts and most of all she needed someone to trust who would hear her heart and try to understand. As the busy signal beeped again, she set the phone down with an impending feeling of loneliness slowly overcoming her. She knew tears were close to the surface and answers seemed so far away.

Her heart ached as she thought of whom she could trust. Whose character was such that she could spill it all and not have to get into the history of every detail? She just wanted to move on, but it seemed so difficult. Before she knew it, she was crying out to the God of her youth. It had been so long since she had thought of Jesus. She remembered her Sunday school teacher so long ago telling her she could call on the name of the Lord and He would save her.

More than a dozen times the Bible tells us when people were in crisis, they would "call on the name of the Lord." The same is true for today. We have power and permission to call on the name of the Lord.

My friends of Jewish ancestry have explained how names possess rich meaning in Hebrew society. In naming a person, place or thing, there would be great thought put into the selection of the name because it needed to represent the attributes and characteristics in one label, a name. There were even ceremonies and rituals associated with naming a child. In announcing the name, they also joyfully read the character qualities associated with the name. Often the parents also revealed why they selected the given name and if there are any ancestral ties within the meaning of the name.

What is your name? What does it say about you as a person? Sister, you have the ability to determine what is associated with your name. You can choose for your name to reflect God's light and love by making sure your actions represent the love of Christ. You can make changes to hold your name in great regard. The book of Proverbs in the Bible tells us a good name is worth more than silver and gold. The Lord even changed Saul's name so he would put away the sinful behavior of his past and take on a new identity in Christ. He became Paul who, through the anointing of God, wrote much of the New Testament of the Bible.

Names also become a powerful indicator when they link with character traits. We can gauge character qualities when we hear someone's name mentioned in a group and others describe character traits saying, "Oh, she is so nice, kind, smart, powerful" and such. Now, I'm not saying all names are an indication of character. Just because you had an aunt who you like, does not mean someone with the same name will earn your trust so quickly. However, if we are in a crowd and we call out the name of a friend, while others may not pay any attention, the friend will come to our calling.

Ladies, it is the same with calling on the name of the Lord. With God, you know you will get consistent character and He will do whatever is necessary to maintain the reputation associated with His name. God's character has been proven over time He will not break a promise. He promises that if you call on Him, He will answer, even if it isn't in the timeframe or manner we expect.

God so desires an intimate relationship with us all. With great confidence, when the battle is raging around you, put down the phone and call on the names of God instead. Calling on His names, based on character, will give you greater tools to fight the enemy's tactics and stand strong in the battle.

Through Christ, we can have a personal relationship with God, so with this list of names we call Him, Our God, and then list the character trait and the name used in the Bible to reveal that promise of character to us. When you are battling the enemy and He seeks to deceive you, call on the specific name of God who keeps promises. You are calling on the same God each time, but you are acknowledging His character and unwavering promises. Additionally, we are letting the enemy know you fully understand the strength of God's names throughout eternity. For example, if you need emotional, physical, and spiritual healing, you can call on Jehovah Rapha.

Names of Our God

Our God, who is the creator, is called **Elohim** (Romans 1:25). When we call on Elohim, it connects us to His glory, majesty and authority. God acts on our behalf with power and might. If you are feeling weakened by life, believe and call on Elohim.

Our God, who is almighty and full of grace, is called **El Shaddai** (Genesis 17:1).The Almighty God makes a covenant with us. The powerful truth is God will not break His covenant with humanity. God desires to be a blessing giver.

Our God, who is the Lord Almighty, is called **Adonai** (Genesis 17:1; Galatians 4:6). Adonai will be our greatest intercessor just as He was with Abraham, as recorded in Genesis 18:3. Proclaim God is a faithful covenant keeper.

Our God, who keeps promises, is called **Jehovah** (Exodus 3:14). Our Jehovah Eternal God is relational and desires intimacy with us. It is never too late to reach out to the Father. He is only a prayer away. Sometimes we are a tear away in communicating with the Lord. He loves you, dear ones. Acknowledge that God will keep His covenant promises to His children.

Our God, who is the most high God and holds everything in His hand and has everything in His control, is called **El Elyon** (Genesis 20:13). It is overwhelming to bathe in the love of God and know that He is the I Am. Receive His assurance that everything is under His sovereignty. Believe that your life does not shock Him. Go to Him unashamed, my sisters. **El Elyon** will never leave or mislead you.

Our God, who is everlasting and unchanging no matter how unstable the world becomes, is called **El Olam** (Genesis 21:33). Stand firm in the truth that no matter what the enemy unleashes in life, depend on God as a constant force in life circumstances. He will not change any of His attributes or promises. That is a comforting truth in times of trial and tribulations.

Our God, who is the shepherd and knows each lamb of the flock, is called **El Rohi** (Psalm 139, Psalm 23:1). As you seek Him, the promises will manifest and become reality in the daily walk. He will guide and direct your path, no matter the journey. As your shepherd, He will walk intimately with you.

Our God, who is all righteousness, is called **Jehovah Tsidkenu** (Jeremiah 23:6). Only through Him can we live righteously. God cannot lie.

Our God, who is the Lord of Hosts, is called **Jehovah Sabbaoth** (Genesis 14:18-22). The Lord wants you to rest in Him. When the burdens are heavy, speak to Him and the load will lighten. Remember we are surrounded by a cloud of heavenly witnesses.

Our God, who will provide all our needs, is called **Jehovah Jireh** (Genesis 22:14). God does not plan for people to lack any good thing that is in accordance with His destiny for each one.

Our God, who heals, is called **Jehovah Rapha** (Exodus 15:22-26). Ask God to heal you emotionally, spiritually and relationally.

Our God, who is peace, is called **Jehovah Shalom** (Judges 6:24). Whenever there is doubt, worry, or anxiety, Jehovah Shalom will show you the path to peace.

Our God, who is always near, is called **Jehovah Shammah** (Ezekiel 48:35). The Hebrew translation of Jehovah Shammah speaks of God's abiding presence, which means to remain and persevere. The Lord desires a daily walk where you are able to rest satisfied under the presence of the Lord.

Chapter 6 *Call on the Names of God ~ Reflection*

1. In what ways have you called on your friends in the past?

2. When you first read the names of God, could you identify a character trait that has been most needed throughout your life? If so, what name do you call on most often?

3. Do you know God will always hear you when you call? He promises to be near. How does that make you feel?

Journal Notes ~ Write your additional thoughts addressing how you see the names of God being a powerful tool in your journey of standing in the battle.

Chapter 7

Ready for Battle

"Finally, be strong in the Lord and in His mighty power. Put on the full armor of God so that you can take your stand against the devil's schemes." (*Ephesians 6:10, NIV*)

As she tugged, twisted and stretched the outfit, it became clear she would not be happy with her reflection in the mirror. She struggled with her view of herself and this wouldn't encourage her self-image. The evening event may mean a promotion or at least a positive image with her co-workers. She needed just the right outfit for this banquet and it seemed nothing fit right. Based on the remarks around the water cooler she knew how easily people label one another as the worst-dressed even if it wasn't true. She understood the reputation could last as long as her career. She wouldn't have any peace knowing company blog sites critique everyone's outfits. She really just desired acceptance for who she was and not to worry so much about the trendy outfits. She wanted to clothe herself in righteousness and an identity of truth, peace, faith and goodness. So, with a sigh of relief, she chose her favorite outfit that represented her style rather than the uncomfortable attire identified by her co-workers as fitting for the event.

S elf-image develops from how we see ourselves. The enemy waits for the opportune time to attack our image, whether it is the one in the mirror or the one in our minds. It is a lot like how the fashion industry would have us make every color "the new black" in each different season and keep us guessing if we are presenting the right image. Now, I enjoy clothes as much as the next girl, but what I am saying is that if our personal image ties to such a superficial thing, we will be caught in another element of the battle with the enemy.

If we chase the industry standards, we may develop a desire to seek validation by our attire. The battle of the mind, as outlined in the book of Ephesians, traps us. We develop a false thought and begin to make decisions based on that foundation. For instance, we may decide that because we need to maintain a fashion standard, it warrants us taking a majority of our paycheck to buy new clothes. If the original false decision remains unchallenged, it can become a habit. Over time if we allow the negative habit to remain, it becomes a stronghold and we become wrapped in bondage. The enemy uses this process of thought, decision, habit and bondage to keep us busy in the battle in any number of areas.

Sisters, here is the good news. God has wardrobe plans that don't change with the seasons and continuously empower us to stand strong in the battle. We can put on the full armor of God. The Bible tells us in the book of Ephesians chapter six to, "put on the full armor of God, so that when the day of evil comes, you may be able to stand your ground, and after you have done everything to stand. Stand firm…"

It goes on to identify the attire of the armor as the belt of truth, breastplate of righteousness, shoes of peace, shield of faith, helmet of salvation and sword of the Spirit, which is the Word of God. These character traits of truth, righteousness, peacefulness and faith will make us stronger and more beautiful than the model on the cover of any magazine. When we are clothed in the armor of God, we take on the character qualities that keep us strong in the battle. Ask God to search your heart, and reveal anything, which will be a hindrance in walking a life of freedom. The very act of asking God to expose any blind spots is a spiritual warfare tool.

Let us look at how each piece of the wardrobe is powerful in our battle gear. The belt of truth prepares us for action as seen in First Samuel chapter 25 verse 13. If truth is first, it holds everything else in place and is foundational. This piece of the armor reminds us to walk in integrity by walking the truth.

A woman's heart is both tender and strong. Women have the capacity to love others and sooth their hurts. The love of a mother to a child is evidence of the balance of strength and softness. The woman's heart is tender, yet encompasses strength beyond compare. You must put on the breastplate of righteousness because Proverbs chapter 4 verse 23 says to keep your heart with all vigilance for out of it flows springs of life. Believe you are made righteous in God's eyes because of the death and resurrection of His son Jesus Christ. Therefore, walk freely in fellowship with God. Be specific when you put on this spiritual armor. Ask God to search your heart and reveal any area the enemy can weaken your armor.

Shoes! Yes, now I have your full attention. I really enjoy a great pair of shoes. They go everywhere and match many outfits. If one has indulged in sweets and not had time to workout, shoes still fit. Shoes are longer lasting than other outfit choices. They seem to be acceptable for more seasons and even white shoes after Labor Day seems to be acceptable now if you wear them with confidence. Therefore, the Bible speaks to us about shoes being part of the armor of God. He tells us to put on the "Gospel Shoes of Peace." It's a good time to ask yourself if where you walk brings peace to the lives and situations of those around you. God promises we can have His peace in all situations. Offensively, this peace will equip you to stand with your feet firmly planted on the Word of God. If you stay planted, you will be unshaken by the enemy's threats and lies. It will protect you to keep steady in the fire of a battle. It will surely keep our spiritual enemy under our feet. It's also interesting that in Exodus chapter 12 God told the people to eat the Passover feast with their shoes on so they would be ready to flee Egypt. We need to know there is peace where we walk, and we need to be ready to leave that place if the Lord leads.

Hats have an interesting history and always make a statement of some kind. The Helmet of Salvation is strong and protects the soldier's head in battle. It gives us eternal perspective so our mind is able to make lasting choices rather than decisions that just fit the day. First Corinthians chapter 2 verse 16 says we have the mind of Christ. Remember, the greatest battlefield is in our minds. We must also expose areas of possible stinking thinking. You know the resentment and bitterness that can creep into thinking over events such as a missed promotion or unjust accusations. The helmet of salvation allows us to guard our minds from impure thinking, doubts and discouragement while we pray for clear focus. Satan will constantly attempt to remind you of failures and negativity in order to destroy your trust in God. Paul reminds us in Philippians chapter 4 verse 8 to focus on things that are true, pure, lovely, of good report and virtue. Guard what we let enter into our minds. Do not let the enemy lower your standards with thoughts like; "You should not get your hopes up. It will not work out anyway." As you immerse yourself in God's Word and prayer, you will develop a discerning mind, which unveils the enemy's subtle tactics. Additionally, historical helmets bore an insignia to identify with which army the soldier fought. This symbol would allow others quickly to identify friend or foe. We must protect our mind and thoughts while knowing what team we represent. The Helmet of Salvation places us on the winning team.

In battle, shields obviously protect soldiers from fiery darts and sharp weapons. Now, the shield of legal officers also helps us identify who is serving to protect us. The Shield of Faith gives us confidence that God will be on the front lines and His character is steady. We can have faith the Lord allows interception of many darts and arrows before they have a chance to reach us. Remember fiery arrows are meant to distract you from the Lord's plans for our lives. Being a follower of Jesus allows you to claim victory and use daily tools to win the battles.

While we don't carry swords in this current day, we can understand that the sword would serve to cut the enemy down in battle. In Ephesians, we see reference to the Sword of the Spirit, which is the word of God. Our sword is to speak the word of God in faith. The Sword of the Spirit serves to defend and offensively attack the enemy by slicing through his lies, so we can rightly divide the truth. Grandmothers, mothers, aunts and friends who seem to see through to the truth of our life are often using the Sword of the Spirit to discern truth. The Sword of the Spirit is one of the most powerful spiritual warfare weapons capable of piercing the darkness of the enemy. Your Sword of the Spirit includes both the power of the Word and the name of Jesus Christ. You will notice there was no armor piece to protect your back. I believe it is because God has our backs covered. Without a consistent prayer life and intimacy with the Father, you will not experience the level of victory you seek.

Yes, the wise woman clothes herself with the armor of God. It always fits, is always appropriate. The Scriptures tells us, you are all daughters of God through faith in Christ Jesus, and were baptized into Christ's family. This means you have clothed yourselves with the armor of victory. We are fully dressed and ready to stand in the battle.

Chapter 7 *Ready for Battle ~ Reflection*

1. In what ways, have you believed a false thought and possibly turned it into actions, habits and finally bondage?

2. When you first read the armor of God, could you identify one piece that is more essential to you than the others? If so, what one and why?

3. Do you know God will always protect you as you wear the armor of God and you will be victorious in battle? How does that make you feel?

Journal Notes ~ Write your additional thoughts and how you see the armor of God being a powerful tool in your journey of standing in the battle.

Chapter 8

Living in Daily Peace

"You, dear children, are from God and have overcome them, because the One who is in you is greater than he who is in the world." *(1 John 4:4)*

Watching the children fly a kite had been invigorating. The colorful kite had lifted slowly at first, then so rapidly, they had to squint to see it dance high above them. The kite had overcome the heavy winds that whirled it side to side or tried to thrust it to the ground. Now, it floated steady, holding the string tight and it would take some muscle to pull it down when the time came.

As the kite decorated the sky, she could see the parallel of her own life. She had a tough time starting out and felt like every choice had been a test. Often she had felt pushed aside or thrust down. With God's help, she had overcome. Things were different now that she trusted God. Yes, it was a different story. She smiled as she watched the confident kite and realized it would also take a lot if anyone tried to pull her down. She was flying on the daily peace of God's loving victory.

Flying above life's circumstances means the enemy has no usable weapons to take you down. We know that no weapon formed against us will prosper. Therefore, we need to make daily choices that influence the peace we have chosen. We must continue to worship and praise God daily while we take a stand in the spiritual battle. In worship, we experience the presence of God. It is as if we invite a hug from our Creator into our lives. When we choose to worship, we are exalting the Lord for who He is. We let Him know if He did not give us anything, we would still worship because He is worthy.

We must also take time to praise God for what He has given us. Praise is a form of thanksgiving that acknowledges the provision of the Lord and that we have an attitude of gratitude. I often think about how God must feel when He chooses to give us something and we ignore Him. We must take time to praise the Living God who gives freely to His children.

Another way to show praise is to remember the blessings of the past. Sister, I understand there is a lot going on in your life. You may be so busy it seems miraculous that you have read this far into a book. However, when it comes to thankfulness, sometimes our memories are short. You need to record and recall the blessings of the past and continue to praise the Lord for them. You must bring to mind the times you have been healed, received financial blessing just in time, or been blessed with a gift you did not expect. You must realize how saving grace protects us from circumstances beyond our control.

One way to remember our blessings is to know we have moved beyond our circumstances. Following a conference, one woman described how she built a shadow box and placed small memorabilia into the display to remember the Lord's provision. Each item became a special positive trigger for her to remember where the Lord helped her overcome life's circumstances. In the Old Testament the Lord gave the Israelites a command to tell the stories of the miracles they received. This memory box helped her tell the stories of how the Lord brought her family through difficult times and into places of daily faith. It allowed her to realize she is more than her circumstances and God is faithful to bring her daily peace even while it seems there are still battles raging around her.

Daily peace does not mean you are always happy. There are times in every woman's life when happiness seems distant. There are times when we have to walk through the consequences of our actions even though we have forgiveness from the original choice. We may still have consequences as a result our choices. Therefore, happiness may seem distant, but we can still experience faithful joy. In fact, we have depth of joy when we choose to pray and read the Bible even when we don't feel like it. In that case, we show the Lord our faithfulness and that means Satan takes notice as well. When we think we aren't getting anything from reading the Bible, it becomes a great time to read it aloud, so the enemy of our souls can hear the truth of God's Word. This process also allows us to replace lies we may have begun to believe with the truth of God's Word.

At the same time, we may recognize how God is faithful to put people in our lives that walk beside us for different seasons. Chances are there are people who hold you accountable and ask just the right question at just the right time. It may be uncomfortable, but God strategically places these people to sharpen you over time. Because they generally do not place harsh judgment on you, it also provides a safe time to begin practicing the art of confession and forgiveness in your life.

While we are worshiping, praising, reading, praying and confessing, we must also take the time to seek heart issues. You may have seeds of doubt, confusion, mistrust or other emotions that could potentially hold you back from God's best in life. Take each issue and follow it to the seed where you began believing a lie. The process allows you to see if there is a seed planted and allowed to take root and grow into a distorted belief system. You must prayerfully ask the Lord to reveal any destructive cycles impeding your freedom walk. The enemy hates this process. He attempts to keep you so busy that you do not make healthy spiritual living a priority.

At first, when we begin to unearth seeds of distortion from our past, it may be uncomfortable and even painful. When clients come to my office, their decision to seek help is often a result of pain. The desire to seek health becomes active when the pain alarm signifies the reality of a problem. Too often, as women, we attempt to stop our children, spouses, friends and family from dealing with pain or consequences of actions. However, God uses pain to help stop harmful thinking, behavior or patterns. When women admit the truth, that there is pain, the journey to wholeness is well underway. Then, you must come face-to-face with yourself and address any areas of distortion. Anything you deny will lengthen your pain. Honesty with yourself will protect you from Satan's deception.

Facing emotional pain can be scary for some women. The thought of taking time to heal seems to feel somewhat selfish. I encourage you to stop, renew your mind, restore and refocus. After facing the truth concerning yourself, others and even God, there is usually a season of grieving the realities. I implore you not to turn away from the grief process, but rather to seek deliverance.

Precious daughters of the King, with each step you take out of pain, you are closer to the clarity and freedom that follows. The resulting freedom will come as you focus on how great it is to be healthy, live in victory and trust the Lord. He will restore the broken places in your life and you will enjoy the view just as the kite that danced on the winds of a clear day. I must add here, if you need to seek professional assistance, do not let the enemy tell you "you don't need help." It is essential to choose to stay in the battle and focus on God's victory plan so you will someday have the awesome honor of standing before the Lord and saying, "I have fought the good fight, and I have finished well." By choosing to live in daily peace, you move beyond your circumstances and stand as a prepared and equipped spiritual soldier.

Chapter 8 *Living in Daily Peace ~ Reflection*

1. In what ways have you chosen to experience daily peace?

2. When you think about possible seeds of deception planted early in your life, can you identify any that could create challenges now? If so, what revelation are you asking God to bring to fullness?

3. Do you know God will always receive your worship and praise? How does that make you feel?

Journal Notes ~ Write your additional thoughts and how you will use the techniques of prayer, praise or reading the Word as a powerful tool in your journey of standing in the battle.

Part III

STANDING VICTORIOUS
IN NEW SHOES

Chapter 9

Step Over the Past and Throw off the Shackles

"You shall know the truth and the truth shall set you free."
(John 8:32)

It was as if she was stepping back in time. She could smell the oven baked macaroni and cheese even while stepping from the car. With each step toward her mother's front porch, the memories would waft over her just as the cheese reminded her of the food bank lines of her childhood. She could hear the sound of the television game shows even before reaching for the screen door. Yes, things seemed so much the same coming home. However, she held her head high and graced a smile of loving freedom as she stepped over the threshold. No, she was very different since she had the truth of God's love in her life. Now, she was able to see her childhood with new eyes. She could respond to the emotional triggers around her and see the positives because her eyes now fixed on her future that is secure in the hope of Jesus Christ. Yes, everything is different now.

Often our memories are longer than we desire. Something that happened in a moment of time will linger with us for the rest of our lives. We may have taken an event and attached meaning to it that is damaging to our lives. In the simplest form, it may have been an aunt who commented that you shouldn't eat so many sweets and she may have even swatted your hand, so you began sneaking the treats. If that moment becomes a self-proclaimed shame message, you may have issues related to sneaking food. You may even find there is an emotional attachment to certain foods and you find it difficult to eat them in front of others.

While this chapter is not about food, you know the kind of issues I mean. For you it may be shopping, procrastination, money, relationships with men or self-damaging messages about your value. Well, it is time to be free. Throw off the shackles of your past hurts, rejection and pain. Sister, you are worth the effort and must take the steps to put on new shoes and step over your past. Dear ones, you must not allow the past triggers to rob you of your potential and the future blessings that come with being a healthy woman. You now have an understanding of the spiritual battle raging around you. You understand the names God calls the enemy and the tactics Satan will try in your life. You have received revelation about God's redeeming power and your ability to call on the names of God while standing in the full armor to live in daily peace regardless of your circumstances. Now, you have the tools you need and are able to stand victorious in new shoes.

We've discussed shoes a couple times in this book, so by now you know how I enjoy a quality pair of fashionable shoes. Ladies, it's tiring seeing women walk around in the same old pair of shoes. Some keep walking where they are comfortable, even if the road leads right back to pain. They wear "shoes of" depression, sadness, discontentment, anger, lust or any number of negative messages. It delights the enemy when we cannot walk forward because we are facing backwards and cannot seem to turn around to see our future.

Today is a victory day. God calls us to walk in victory, so we must step over our past with new shoes that reflect our new life and our future. Yes, we can still recognize an emotional trigger. When this happens, we get a quick check in our heart that some familiar emotion, is kicking up its heels. However, there is power in the recognition. We are able to say to ourselves, yes, I remember how it felt when that happened. I also know I took the time to heal. You can ask yourself if there are any unresolved issues. Are there areas you need to address, things left unsaid, tasks that need completing based on the original emotional event? If you have already done the work and given the healing to the Lord, then you can smile, recognize the trigger and step over the event.

Surprise! It is the old abusive boyfriend sitting at Mom's house. That is a big trigger, so what do you do? Say hello, walk in your new shoes standing tall, recognize the past is over and move forward. You may even have reason to praise the Lord for His loving protection from past choices. Also, remember it is not a good idea to try to rekindle an abusive relationship. It is often just a way to be burned.

Now that you understand what an emotional trigger is and how you can move quickly past it, you must step into a place of renewal. When you step over your past, it's essential that you set your feet on a firm foundation of God's plans for you. The Heavenly Father's love is solid and secure. You can set your stance in His direction. This knowledge is a key to our renewal process. You may need to surround yourself with new friends who build you up rather than tear you down. You may need to remove some of the triggers of your past and surround yourself with the positive triggers such as the shadow box we previously discussed. Find things that remind you of your healing, the Holy Spirit's power and God's provision in your life.

While you are stepping over your past with your new shoes, you will want to take on behaviors that positively reflect God's healing. I have identified a shoe selection of qualities we can wear to step over our past and walk in victory. You may decide to look up the Bible verses and use your journal to expand on these thoughts.

Every well-suited sister must have two shoes. It would look funny to walk wearing only one shoe. It takes a matching pair to walk in harmony. It generally takes two shoes to go farther than one alone. We are supposed to walk together in relationship. Romans 16:16 tells us to greet one another. I believe we need to do this like the sandals we wear. We need to be relaxed, comfortable and open. We also need both a right and left shoe to make a pair. They are never quite the same, so it is important to be at peace with each other (Mark 9:50).

When we are running fast, having comfortable and supportive shoes is vital. It's a lot like tennis shoes where we feel supported and can move quickly. We put on tennis shoes and play in the relationship game by serving one another in love (Galatians 5:13).

Whereas high heels may make us feel taller and more confident, it's essential we use that feeling to build each other up (1Thessalonians 5:11). While we are walking alongside others, we may need to put on our boots to walk through the muck of life. At this point, we need to carry each other's burdens by coming alongside your sister until she can take her own steps (Galatians 5:2).

We also need to make sure we have our comfortable slippers. We need to be patient, bearing with one another, and ourselves, in love and honesty (Ephesians 4:2).

Finally, in our shoe selection, we must have a great pair of dancing shoes and enjoy the music of life as we boogie, glide, laugh and enjoy the fun. We must dance together as it says in John 13:34 to "Love one another." Sisters, it is time to dance! The play on words is a fun way to remind you that when you step over the past, you can do it with style and that the Lord turns your mourning into dancing if you allow His love to permeate your every fiber. You are more than victorious when you pick up the tools you are given, and use them to tell the enemy you understand his tactics, but instead choose God's plans for your life.

The actual shoes you wear are not important. It is the attitude in which you walk that matters. Where you walk, you have the power to bring blessings, joy and peace to the area. Some of the most beautiful women I have met had the most wonderfully decorated shoes. Others had no shoes and walked the dusty roads in Africa. They greeted me with hugs, and their smiles radiated the joy of the Lord.

During my first trip to Africa, a sister-in-Christ blessed me with a beautiful piece of fabric. She took my measurements and by the end of the ministry trip, she had fashioned a gorgeous new outfit especially for me. I was awestruck how she had used the tools she had to create something so beautiful out of what previously was flat fabric. She used what she knew. She had her tools, worked diligently and created a new garment for me to put on for a final dance at the conference conclusion. She added to the joy of the journey. Like her, we must use what we know, pick up our tools and work diligently to stand strong with victory in the battle.

Chapter 9 *Stepping Over the Past ~ Reflection*

1. In what ways have you experienced triggers from your past?

2. When you think about emotional triggers, are you going through the process of dealing with them quickly? If so, what revelation is God giving you about your emotional health?

3. Do you know you can walk in new shoes and stand victoriously? How does that make you feel?

Journal Notes ~ Write your additional thoughts and how you will use an understanding of emotional triggers to put on new shoes and stand facing your future in Christ.

Chapter 10

Hear God's Voice

"Consequently, faith comes from hearing the message, and the message is heard through the word of Christ." *(Romans 10:17 NIV)*

She jolted awake as the plane turbulence went from rocking to that of a bumpy road. Glancing at her watch she realized she would be changing it again as they passed into another time zone. Her physical body was tired, but spiritually she was very alert from her time with the amazing women of Africa. Did she really need to leave the trappings of the United States to have such spiritual awaking? She supposed not, but knew this journey had been one where she had so clearly heard the Lord because the women put away all selfish desires and sought only the heart of Father God. It had been transforming to tune-in so clearly to hear God's heart for each woman.

I laughed as my friend recounted how she just wanted God to leave her a little fridge magnet telling her what to do. She desperately wanted to hear from God while she was making a tough decision that would affect her future career. That same day, her child found a fridge magnet and placed it centrally for Mom to find while making dinner. The magnet simply stated "Trust God."

Sometimes we desire an audible voice from heaven to tell us exactly what to do. While God could let us know with a booming voice what our next steps should be, He prefers to honor our free will and speak in the still small voice of everyday surroundings. When you daily read the Bible, pray and develop sensitivity to the things of God, you will be amazed how much you hear God's plans for your life.

You do not have to leave your community to hear the voice of God. In fact, you may need to hear God's heart for your own community so you can better serve and bring freedom right where you are now.

When it comes to standing in the battle, you now have a lot of information about how to discern what is from Satan or from God. It takes some practice, but over time it becomes very clear how God's voice will always match His character. Therefore, when you are unsure if you are hearing from the Lord, you can go back to the basics of lining the message up with the messenger. If you know God's character, you know He will not direct you to do something that goes against His nature. Therefore, God will never tell you to speak falsely, cheat or any such behaviors to get ahead.

One of the scenarios I have seen is when a young couple is ready to purchase a home. They believe they have heard from God that it is time and the house they are looking at just seems so perfect for them. However, when they are completing the loan documents they find they will have to make false statements about their income in order to get in the home. They may even decide to borrow from family to have enough for the down payment. However, this would not be God's plan, even if it seems like it would make the couple happy. God would never promote false information as a way to get where you want to go. If the couple purchases the home, it could cause undue hardship on their finances, and their marriage. They may find there are unseen circumstances that happen and then are tied to a house they were never intended to have. If they choose not to purchase the home, God could use the circumstance to promote perseverance and He may have a better deal just around the corner for them if they will stand in honesty and wait for God's perfect timing.

God always has a calm approach and will never shout us down or cause confusion. He is not the author of confusion. Throughout the Bible, we read about God's love being like that of a shepherd who leads His sheep. When sheep are eating their grass in the field, they tend to stay in the flock so they feel safe. If the shepherd approaches with a gentle voice, the sheep will follow and stay in safety. However, the enemy approaches to bring chaos and scatter the sheep so he can get the weaker ones away from the protection of the flock. The Good Shepherd, God, has a quiet and internal voice. When you rest in His love and seek quietness, you will discern the calm still voice of your Lord. Although, I admit, there were times when God had to blow the trumpet to get my attention.

It is essential to read the Bible because God's voice will always agree with revelation about Him in the Scriptures. There are no contradictions in the Bible and there are no contradictions in God's character. God's Word is full of grace, mercy, love and forgiveness. Therefore, if you are sensing shame, condemnation and doubt, God is not the author of the message. In fact, the enemy distorts truth just the same as he did in heaven, in the garden and in the wilderness as we previously discussed.

God's voice will focus our attention on our growth and character development with a look toward the future rather than the past. He tells us throughout scripture that He has a future and a hope for us that will not bring us harm. Dear ones, regardless of our weaknesses and imperfections, our Abba Father adores us. God says, "Yes, I have loved you with an everlasting love; therefore with loving kindness I draw you" (Jeremiah 31:3).

It is also an indication of God's voice if the effect is one of freedom from bondage, peace even in storms and hope for the hopeless. When we listen to God's voice, we will become more empathetic and drawn to helping others find the same hope we have in Christ.

Chapter 10 *Hear God's Voice ~ Reflection*

1. In what ways have you heard God's voice in your life?

2. When you think about God's character and how He speaks to you, can you identify trends that help you hear him better? If so, what are they?

3. Do you know God desires to speak to you personally in a still small voice and wants you to discern His voice from the pull of the world? How does that make you feel?

Journal Notes ~ Write your additional thoughts and how you will develop habits that allow you to better hear God's voice for your life.

Chapter 11

Walk in Freedom

"But the fruit of the Spirit is love, joy, peace, patience, kindness, goodness, faithfulness, gentleness and self control." *(Galatians 5:22)*

During her pregnancy, she read every parenting magazine, booklet and catalogue. Her nursery was well-decorated and her friends piled on the advice. However, when the baby arrived, it surprised her how difficult things seemed. Now she was tired, irritable and unsure of her new life. She realized quite quickly that the baby had not read any of the same material and what she believed should have come naturally was actually very difficult for her. One night as the baby seemed to cry continuously, the young mom had an overwhelming sense of love for this little life. She felt the joy of being a mom and had patience beyond what she ever thought she could experience. She experienced peace even when she was so tired. Yes, she had been praying, loving and going through the motions of meeting daily needs, but this was an entirely new sense of God's grace. At that moment she realized she was experiencing the fruit of the Spirit because she laid down all she thought things should be based on her reading of popular material and she allowed God to bless her prayers with the freedom to be the Mom she was created to be in that moment.

When you walk as a restored person who loves the Lord and listens to God's plans for your life, the fruit of the spirit is evident. There are no limits to what He can and will do for those who seek Him. When you walk, others even notice there is more love in the room. You bring joy on your journey and peace even where there was turmoil. You have more patience and kindness toward those who have not received such things in a long time. You are faithful, gentle and self-controlled.

Sisters, I know it sounds too good to be true, but it is the mighty truth of God. You can only experience the fullness of the fruit when you walk in freedom. Notice, you were standing in the battle, but now you are walking. You have stepped out, stepped up and stepped over your past. You have the tools you need to walk in freedom and experience the fullness of the fruit of the Spirit. Here's the thing, it's not the fruits, plural. It's not like a fruit bowl where you can select one without the other. You cannot choose to have the love part without the self-control part. It does not work that way because it's all one part of the character God gives. When we see God in someone's life, the fruit is evident.

Therefore, it's essential you use the fruit of the Spirit as a gauge for how you are doing in your new shoes. It must be obvious that there is fruit from your efforts. People will notice the excellence that surrounds you. In addition, you will be expectant of great things. You will walk with the expectancy that God is planning a holy assignment for you. You will look forward rather than back.

The enemy will try to find ways to discourage you on this journey. He may even choose to use people around you. It can be challenging when those around you begin to speak discouragement in your life. They may point out your past failures and tell you all the reasons you won't succeed. This kind of person keeps pointing out your past and won't let it pass. Therefore, you must continue to walk in your healing and restoration. You can acknowledge who you were and tell people how you have changed. If you were abused, accused, misused, you have a story that will bring light to others. Understanding the past reveals knowledge about patterns, behaviors and beliefs, which can bewilder us in the present and affect the future. So, you can remember your past without claiming the labels it contains. Instead of saying, "I am an abused woman," you must say, "I am a restored woman." There is true freedom when we speak truth to those around us. Restoration brings courage to live in freedom. We are free to be forgiven and to forgive others. We are free to let go of false expectations of self, others and God. Freedom allows us to rise up to our fullest potential as daughters of the Lord.

Yes, people are watching how you live as a transformed person. They are watching your priorities, balance and boundaries to see if you live what you speak. Over time as they see the fruit of the Spirit in your life, they will decide your integrity is genuine. Know that there will always be people who will continue to remind you of your past. It is essential you remember you are not living with excellence so they will see your change, but you are living with excellence so they will see all God has done. Colossians chapter two verses 23, 24 says, "Whatever you do, work at it with all your heart, as working for the Lord, not for men, since you know that you will receive an inheritance from the Lord as a reward. It is the Lord Christ you are serving."

This is especially important to remember when you are quietly serving or if you faithfully work for years and seem to receive no solid recognition. You do not need to worry who sees, because God is watching your faithfulness. The enemy would delight in tripping you up by casting doubt into your service. Watch for areas where you are tempted to feel slighted, passed over or resentful that no one recognizes the time and energy you spend serving. You must immediately combat that attitude with encouragement of the truth. The truth is that God sees all and values the servant heart working with a spirit of excellence for His purposes rather than personal gain. This does not mean God does not want you to prosper.

In many success seminars, people discuss the principle of beginning any task or journey with the end in mind. It makes sense to know where you want to pitch your tent before you begin the road trip. The same can be true for this time on earth. We have the power to develop our legacy. You can largely create the statements about you when you are gone. A friend who studied print journalism tells of her first college news writing assignment where the students were required to write their own obituary. It was a practical lesson beyond writing but one that identified priorities and gave a goal that began with the end in mind and created an opportunity to design a life message.

It is essential for you to know yourself as well as the enemy knows you. My sisters, understand the inroads that rob your peace, steal your joy and destroy your destiny. God will divinely instruct you and provide all wisdom to walk restored. You must learn to walk in new skin after the healing process. God will fight the battle. It is your responsibility to learn the needed tools to demystify the warfare. As you have already read, inroads can be anything from critical judgmental thoughts to traumatic events. Other inroads may have developed from a label that stuck over time. Satan intimidates and sneers at our confidence and causes disbelief of the truth and promises of God. Sisters, continue to fill up on the freshness of the Holy Spirit and do not rely on yesterday's filling. God is truly faithful.

In 1962, I wrote in my Bible the words I desire on my tombstone. It will read, "I have fought the good fight, I have run the race, I have kept the faith." That verse in Second Timothy chapter 4 verse 7 sums up the result of a life serving the Lord, enjoying the fruit of the Spirit, and continually standing victoriously while battling the enemy of our souls. When you walk through the spiritual battles and live as a restored woman, you can experience great joy in the journey. Congratulations on living your life with great expectations that God will continue to do miracles in, through and around you.

Chapter 11 *Walk in Freedom ~ Reflection*

1. In what ways have you experienced the Fruit of the Spirit?

2. When you think about your obituary, what will people remember about you?

3. Do you know God desires for you to walk in complete freedom and expect holy assignments along your journey? How does that make you feel?

Journal Notes ~ Write your additional thoughts and determine what you want engraved on your tombstone at the end of your life on earth.

Chapter 12

Equipped with New Tools

"She sets about her work vigorously; her arms are strong for her tasks." *(Proverbs 31:17 NIV)*

Although she couldn't remember the words that filled the air of the graduation speech, she easily recalled the feeling of the satiny robe with flowing sleeves as she reached for the long-awaited award. Even now, she could almost feel the odd shaped mortar hat perched on her head with the tassel hanging within view. She had worked tirelessly and overcome many odds to get there. Now, she would hold her head high and begin the work for which she trained. Yes, she had the tools she needed for success and now it was time to use what she learned along the way. Although she couldn't recall each specific fact of her training, she knew all the time and energy had compiled to give her what she needed to move forward.

Whether you have formal training or not, you have experience that allows you to be an expert. You know yourself, your history, your experiences, your strengths and your weaknesses. You also know God has a plan for your life and you know the enemy is battling to rob that plan from you. Now is your opportunity to take what you know and bring victory to your life and those who come along your path. It's time to work vigorously and know the Lord will make you strong for your tasks.

Ladies, it's time to check the tool box and see what you need to grab onto to be ready for the work ahead. We are going to look at some key characteristics you must have ready for greater effectiveness in using what you have learned.

First is "Commitment." The enemy pulls out all stops to prevent you from flowing in your anointing. He attempts to immobilize you and keep you from using your spiritual gifts. If God gives you a task to do, you must be committed to the task until it's time to stop. When you are committed, others see the excellence in the way you work. For example, if there's a team getting ready to do something exciting, there are people who join in the excitement when they first hear about the work. However, they seem to disappear when the tasks move from play to action. It can be frustrating to serve as a committed Christian and have others seem to flake out, but as you stay committed, the Lord will give you assignments fitted to your level of excellence. You must stay committed to your course regardless of the journey others are taking. This attitude exemplifies commitment. Psalm 37:5 tells us to "Commit everything you do to the Lord. Trust Him to help you do it, and He will."

We must also stay "Creative." This is where you get out of the box and find new ways of doing things. The Bible tells us there is nothing new under the sun. That does not mean we can't try something that is new to us or to the way others function. It gets tiring working with people who continually refer to the way things "have always been done." We need to be fresh and allow the whole picture of who we are to develop to its fullest. Isaiah 43:17 reminds us that God loves doing new things in our lives and He is never stagnant.

In talking with pastor's wives, one of the common themes is the feeling they are living life in a fishbowl. Everyone has expectations of who she is and how she should behave. Have you ever seen a gold fish in a small fishbowl? It seems to stay small and not outgrow the fish bowl. If you take the same goldfish and place it in a pond, the goldfish will often grow larger than the previous bowl. It is time to expand the fishbowl. Be creative and allow others to see you live your life with the creativity God designs. Yes, this may involve making a few mistakes, but grow through those areas of discomfort and begin to sparkle more as you grow.

We also must have "Concrete Expectations" of ourselves. The Lord took the time for us to have His words in writing. Habakkuk, chapter two verse two, says we must write the visions down. When we put our vision in writing, we are able to refer to it when we may not feel the same about the daily tasks it will take to achieve our vision. We can go to our toolbox and refer to the concrete expectations we have and it leads to greater focus for our lives.

"Continuity" and "Clarity" are vital in our development of integrity. People need to know they can continuously count on us for excellence. When we remain in a ministry, job or family role and serve with continuity, it develops a level of trust with those around us. We also have the ability to pick up many tools along the way that add clarity to our journey. Clarity is essential so we are purposeful about why we are serving. The tasks involved in everyday life can become drudgery unless we have clarity as to why we are doing them. Changing a baby's diaper is no particular joy, until you have clarity of the love for that child and you experience the continuity that builds relational trust.

When you are using the tools you learn, you are cultivating your character. It is essential you remain a lifelong learner who receives teaching, correction and guidance from other trusted followers of Jesus Christ. Once we cultivate relationships that build us up, it becomes easy to discern who has our interest at heart and whom God is using to add value to your journey.

As you prayerfully consider the tools in your toolbox, realize you are able to pull out the techniques needed when you face each challenge. If you have never faced a certain challenge you may be easily pushed out of balance. However, because you know the Lord has tools available for you to use, you can ask for help. Often God will place someone around you who has gone through similar trials to share her tools with you until you are able to add to your own toolbox. For that very reason, it is important to be authentic and available to those around you. A word of caution: maintain healthy boundaries so you do not burn out doing good things versus God's best.

Remember, you are walking in victory and can be real about the challenges you have faced. You have overcome them and can share the tools developed along the way with others. If you are in a place where others try to shame you, leave that place. Even Jesus shook the dust from His sandals and went to a new town where He was welcomed. Sisters, do not stay where you feel merely tolerated. Go where you are celebrated. Use your new tools to continue building your character and get strong in your ability to stand victoriously in the battle.

Chapter 12 *Equipped with New Tools ~ Reflection*

1. In what ways, have you used some of the tools discussed in the chapter?

2. Consider your character development in areas of commitment, continuity, creativity, clarity and concrete expectations. Are there areas you need prayerful consideration for personal growth? If so, how will you develop those areas?

3. Do you know God desires your character growth more than He is concerned about your comfort? How does that make you feel?

Journal Notes ~ Write your additional thoughts and how you will develop your personal toolbox so you are ready for the battle when the next challenge arises.

Conclusion

Living Victoriously in Christ

"I have fought the good fight, I have run the race, and I have kept the faith." *(2 Timothy 4:7)*

The conference had been amazing. Women continuously asked for more information. The majority of women stepped into freedom and gained understanding how to walk in victory. It was awesome! She turned to her friend and said, "We have to get this into print and multiply the message the Lord has given." With full agreement the sisters-in-Christ set out on a journey of prayer, meetings, late nights, early mornings, writing, editing, researching and seeking the Lord until at last the Lord said to each, "It is finished." He took the work, multiplied the efforts, released His healing and took their efforts places beyond their dreams. It became evident God would take the text and empower women of His choosing.

The truth shall set you free. As you examine any of the chains that seek to bind you up, you can unlock each link with the truth as presented in God's Word. Congratulations on taking the journey to full freedom and understanding of the spiritual battle that surrounds us. As you use what you have read, continue to seek God's plans for your life. We close the book as we began; with an understanding that God is victorious and plans for us to be more than conquerors through Christ.

To finish well, we must maintain an eternal perspective about our lives. We must look beyond our todays and seek brighter tomorrows through intimacy with our loving God. Sister, you can do all things through Christ who strengthens you. You are a mighty woman of God. You are a woman of destiny who may have a gift as a prophet, evangelist, handmaiden, teacher, warrior, discerner, faith-builder, exhorter, truth and wisdom speaker or servant. You are a child of God, living in a called generation. God summons you to bear witness to the great things He does in your life. Press on, in and through the battles with the divine assistance from heaven. Esther 4:14 tells how ordinary women can be called, sent and commissioned to accomplish extraordinary things for kingdom sake. May you recognize your season, prepare for the purpose and act boldly in the appointed time.

Daughter of the King, continue to walk in all authority, all wisdom, all anointing, all courage, and all boldness. Receive from your Heavenly Father and allow Him to bless and daily enrich your life. Stand secure knowing your identity is wrapped in who God says you are. The Lord promises He will meet your needs. He will protect your soul and mind. He will tenderly cover your heart and bring you comfort and peace that will surpass anything you have ever known. The Lord will be your hiding place, shelter, refuge and strong tower.

The Father has dreams and visions for you, His daughter. Walk on, my sister. Speak, live, and share truth, struggles and victories with other sisters. Tell others your adversity trains, refines and strengthens your character. Mighty woman of God, I pray you will be a light in dark places of the world.

Be a champion and an anointed vessel for Jesus' sake. Run the race faithfully and diligently. Run the race in your unique style and do not compare yourself to others. Run with all humility, yet boldly. Practice and use the keys of spiritual warfare you have acquired.

God tells us our design is for His purpose. Wherever you are, you are ready to release your visions and dreams. You are beloved and precious jewels in the eyes of your Abba Father. He adores you and seeks to lavish on you. No matter where you have been or what you have done, God loves you. As His daughter, you are the apple of your Heavenly Father's eye. God is the I Am. Sister, you are on the winning side. Adversity has no hold on you, so rise from darkness victoriously. Walk in authority, power, faith and truth. The time is now. You, who are ready for the call, shout and rejoice in the Lord. You are highly favored and dearly loved.

This is your day, hour, moment, and season. I say to you, this is a time to break the shackles of your past. It is time to break the chains of bondages and pull down strongholds through the Power of the Holy Spirit. Declare this day the revelations of the Lord for the next level of God's anointing, healing, deliverance and blessing are on the way. Your prayers are eternal if spoken in accordance with the will and promises of the Lord. So, do not hold back. God's grace has, and will, keep you through all of life's dramas. The best is yet to come. Before the foundations of the world, God looked forward to your season. The Bible instructs us to write the God-revealed visions and make it plain upon the tablets that you may run with it at the appointed time. Wait patiently, even when it seems long. God is never late. He knows the divine purpose for your life. Walk on, my sisters, you can stand tall, strong and ready in the battle.

"For though we live in the world, we do not wage war as the world does. The weapons we fight with are not the weapons of the world. On the contrary, they have divine power to demolish strongholds. Casting down arguments and every high thing that exalts itself against the knowledge of God. Bringing every thought into captivity to the obedience of Christ." *(2 Corinthians 10:3-5)*

"Your ears shall hear a word behind you saying, this is the path, now walk in it." (Isaiah 30:21) Where we walk is Holy ground.

~ Amen

Addendum

Personal Surrender to God's Sovereignty

"He has sent me, Jesus, to heal the brokenhearted . . . and to set at liberty those who are bruised." (Luke 4:18)

As a Christian African-American woman, she antici-pated many challenges as she planned the ministry trip into the heavily Muslim country. It would be an honor to teach at the University, but even more, she sensed the anticipa-tion of God using the opportunity to bring freedom to many. When the call came also to speak at a global conference during the travel, she was nearly overwhelmed at the privi-lege. Because she knew her calling to equipping others to live free, fruitful lives, she was prepared for the challenge. As the hours multiplied, it seemed the plane would never land, but the trip fatigue mixed with excitement at the plans for an evening dinner with the ministry team and University leaders. The cold bit to the core as the team made their way from the airport to where they would spend the next weeks. As she carried her luggage in the dark hallway, the light they could bring to the spiritual darkness struck her.

They were providing a spiritual threshold for change. As she crossed over the physical threshold, she tripped on the elevated doorway. When her shoe caught in the groove of the wood, it held-fast as she crashed to the floor. Ultimately, the pop from her knee echoed the pain in her heart. She had a sinking feeling that the trip of a lifetime had changed the rest of her life. In a span of five seconds while half way around the world from home, her life had changed forever and she had not yet had an opportunity to even speak.

Her mind filled with questions. Was this part of God's plan? How would God fulfill His plan? How would she gracefully get through the trip, support the team and still serve the Lord? How will she accept God's Sovereignty in the midst of this adversity? It would take several weeks, multiple countries and prayer across the continents to bring her home. Yes, the damage appeared permanent and, unless the Lord miraculously intervened, she would now do ministry with a leg brace or wheel chair, but the journey of a lifetime would ultimately influence a multitude of lives.

I am sure, at one time or another, all of us experience circumstances that alter the course of our lives. It does not matter whether the storms of life result from death, divorce, physical illness, injustice, betrayal, or a natural disaster, they are painful. Some storms roll-in with no warning. Shaken to the core, we have to change our thinking. Throughout my family history, physical pain and trauma have knocked at our doorstep. Cancer and other forms of physical illnesses took both a sister and brother. Both of them died at the age of 29-years-old. In 2005, my precious mother died only six weeks after a cancer diagnosis. The very same week, my other brother experienced rupture within his spinal cord, which left him paralyzed from the chest down.

Satan tries repeatedly to weaken me spirituality through the vulnerability of physical challenges. I still stand through many life-shaking, faith-testing, and surrendering walks with my Lord. During these times, we must see the blessings of the Lord and retain the lessons we learn. We learn those lessons as we walk step-by-arduous-step through life's sufferings and dark moments of despair. Yes, the desert is a place where we come face-to-face with our Lord and with ourselves. It is a place where, at last, we say, "I can't do this. You take over, Lord." When we have a need greater than our abilities, knowledge, talents and spiritual gifts, God releases a miracle. As we send prayers up towards heaven, blessings come down. In writing this book, I pray you are uplifted as I address one last spiritual warfare tool. You must be willing to surrender to our Sovereign God in the midst of adversity. You can practice all the spiritual disciplines and still experience trails and tribulations. In desolate seasons, Satan does not want us to yield and live under the protective wings of the Almighty God.

I pray, as you read this you will decide to obediently walk this earthly journey, and your testimony will be one of honesty, love, grace and faithfulness to your Sovereign Abba Father. You have already read what you need to understand, know and act upon to stand in the battles. I know we dare not lack needed wisdom to advance in the midst of adversity.

Understanding God's sovereignty means we must settle some questions. Ladies, how do we respond when a ton of bricks hits us with a life-altering situation? The questions about God's sovereignty will rise from our souls and cry out for answers. This normal response occurs when the situation just does not make sense. Nonetheless, we must come to terms with God's sovereignty and learn to surrender to Him, while courageously walking through our suffering. Understanding how means we need a definition of sovereignty as it relates to spiritual warfare. The clarity, I hear from the Holy Spirit, is to tell you, God says, "I Am the I Am." In studying the Bible, meditating, and praying, I see that the I Am is all encompassing. He is Elohim, the Sovereign God, who is our creator. There are no other God's before Him. That is sovereign.

Then we ask, what does God's sovereignty cover? From the Lord, the answer is so simple; we may miss the still, small voice. However, He speaks distinctly in saying, "Everything" my daughter. Yes, sisters, everything is under the sovereignty of God, including our suffering. Everything that happens to us, Gods loving watch permits. Through the dark times, I have learned the spiritual discipline of giving it all to God. I surrender with a statement, "Even this, I give to you."

When you are hurting, this is often very difficult. It is tempting to angrily question how God could allow such terrible things in your life. While I understand this, I cannot speak for all circumstances. However, I know the truth is that God is sovereign, and each of us has a uniquely personal journey that God allows to shape us with more Christ-like character. None of us knows the shape we need to reach our full destiny, prepared for us even before the foundations of this world. However, from the beginning of adversity to full release of the situation brings us full circle in our spiritual warfare journey.

When adversity strikes, we may try to cope and desperately search for ways to bring equilibrium back into lives. However, sometimes there is nothing we can do to change the reality; our lives will never be the same again. Now, we must learn to rise out of our pain, confusion and defeatist mentality. Those who are not aware of the enemy's ability to capitalize on these circumstances entangle in a web of despair, despondency, fear, bitterness, and disillusionment. That is a terribly powerless place where people become victims in their own lives. To transition out of this bleak place, we must know the attributes, characteristics and promises of our sovereign God. Sister, God hears the tenderness of our hearts and He finds a way to remind us we are not forsaken.

Throughout this book, you learned to take control of thoughts that could potentially lead you on a path of despair. You know it is a struggle to stay strong when your thoughts are under attack. We must remember Satan is not all knowing, all-present, or all-powerful. Satan can do nothing without the permission of our sovereign God. The enemy cannot defeat us, unless we allow it.

Adversities come into all our lives and our attitude either creates a crisis in confidence or strengthens us to rise to new levels. Isaiah 48:10 says we are refined, but not in the way silver is refined, rather, we refine in the furnace of suffering." Our sovereign God loves us enough to bring us to places of maturity, even through pain. When we live through challenge, we may not feel like things are ordinary, but I assure you it is ordained.

God says in Ephesians chapter two verse 10; we are designed for the good works He has prepared in advance. God did not say review all the options and think about doing good things. Instead, He said to walk in it. The Lord did not tell us to wait until the storm is over. He wants us to be confident and triumph in the midst of all chaos breaking out around us. These are times to connect with Father God from a revelation perspective and walk in obedience. While traveling internationally, I discovered it does not matter if you are in a third-world country, or your own backyard, when it comes to facing the enemy of our souls, there is only one God, only one Jesus, only one Holy Spirit and only one Satan. The way Satan attacks you in one country or another may be different culturally, but the tactics are the same. God wants you to walk through adversity feeling prepared, secure and confident.

It's clear there are many different adversities in life because this world fell from grace. Many times, I counseled people who came so close to victory. I could see how God was ready to deliver them over the hump, when fear, doubt or shame overcame them and they stopped the process of restoration. In times of suffering, if we dare stop running, we may miss the crest of our miracle. We must stay focused in the battle. The truth is, life will knock us down on the outside, but we must get up on the inside.

Enduring adversity will certainly test our faith. Now, if we allow the suffering to complete its work in us, we will develop perseverance. As we press-on, the outcome leads to maturity and stability. A stable mind stays strong with every storm. The book of James encourages us to ask God for wisdom when we do not know what to do in times of suffering. Go to God in your weakness and pain. Our experiences will make us more compassionate. The challenges we live through teach us to be resourceful, self-disciplined, patient, grateful and courageous.

While we are going through the trials, the Lord is merciful to take us through the journey. He still provides grace and because He is sovereign, delivery is on the way at the perfectly appointed time. That is sovereignty in motion. My mother used to say how adversity is part of life and since you will not get out of this world alive, you have to find the path to become victorious and overcome today's adversity. Help will be available while we walk in-and-out of the journey. We have an intercessor in Heaven, who is Jesus the Christ. When you feel you cannot make it, do not follow your feelings. Instead, activate your faith and step with truth, wisdom and power. The power to deal with adversity is the same power that raised Jesus from the dead.

God is still on the throne and indeed, He is sovereign. Precious ones, it is a guarantee; He will not give us more than we can bear. This means together with God, you choose the side that ultimately wins the war.

About the Author

Credentials:

- BSN in Behavioral Science and Nursing
- MA in Theology and Biblical Counseling
- Certification in Chemical Dependence
- Certified Grief Specialist
- Certified Human Behavior Consultant
- Member of a variety of advisory boards in both a pastoral and professional capacity

Dee Brown is the founder and executive of Cornerstone Coaching, a multi-purpose enterprise with a unique ministry focus on the "journey to wholeness" and an outreach focus on equipping. Her trainings assist groups and individuals to excel and experience passionate and victorious living.

Dee is the co-founder of EducateSuccess, an international organization providing a transformational program designed to eliminate barriers, which prevent personal and professional success.

Dee inspires people to reach beyond seeming impossibilities. She has been a pastoral ministry consultant and trainer since 1978. As an adult educator, she taught in the community colleges and state prisons systems where she developed various programs addressing addictions, grief, and re-entry after incarceration.

Dee is a retired nursing administrator in the medical and mental health fields. She has received many accolades, and is most pleased with being named "Nurse of the Year" three separate times by her peers in Washington State. She authored a variety of training materials addressing spiritual, relational and emotional health.

A multi-cultural understanding allows Dee to work as an organizational strategist in diverse communities, both culturally and multi-denominationally. As a seasoned international and national trainer, Dee has a reputation for her down-to-earth style, candid presentation and sense of humor.

She is a founding board member of several organizations that all serve as ministry resources and training networks. Dee's passion is to mobilize, and equip churches in becoming safe, transforming and restorative communities nationally and internationally. Dee's goal is to pass on a ray of hope regardless of a person's circumstances and provide an opportunity for people to be free to pursue their God-given destiny.

To contact the author, please write:

Cornerstone Coaching, Dee Brown 11417 124th Ave NE ~
Suite 202 Kirkland, WA 98033

DB.Cornerstone@verizon.net

Please include your story, or the help you received from this book, when writing. You may also request a conference schedule or purchase a workbook in conjunction with this material. Your prayer requests and praise reports are always welcome.

Printed in the United States
77769LV00001B/1-201